DIG YOURSELF OUT OF DEBT

HOW TO REDUCE AND ELIMINATE YOUR DEBT FOR A LIFE OF FINANCIAL FREEDOM

CHRISTOPHER KESSLER

&

MICHAEL MORTORANO

CHRISTOPHER KESSLER & MICHAEL MORTORANO

ISBN: 1482577097
ISBN-13: 978-1482577099

This book is dedicated to Kristen Loren.

DIG YOURSELF OUT OF DEBT

INTRODUCTION

The purpose of this book is to identify and explain the options available to every consumer through various debt hardship, elimination, reduction, and relief programs. Finance, credit, collections, debt management, and debt settlement professionals are well informed about how credit is extended and collected. Michael and I combined have more than 25 years of knowledge and experience in the finance, credit, collections, and debt settlement industries. This book is a comprehensive effort to teach you, the consumer, how to effectively evaluate your current financial situation and determine the best course of action to reduce and eliminate your debt.

Because most consumers are not familiar with how interest and finance charges are applied to their credit account or they aren't aware of the programs offered by creditors to consumers with financial hardships, we have included descriptions of various hardship programs, along with step-by-step instructions on how to contact your creditors to effectively negotiate and reduce your debt. In the appendix, we have included example letters that can be used when contacting creditors and negotiating your accounts. We've also included financial and budget-planning worksheets for managing your budget.

For those consumers with a financial hardship, we hope to offer a broad overview of debt relief programs, with an emphasis on how you, the consumer, can effectively negotiate your own debt without having to hire a professional and pay hundreds or even thousands of dollars in fees.

Our goal for consumers without a hardship yet overwhelmed with debt is to provide an overview of an accelerated debt elimination plan that can take the average family with 30 years of debt to being debt-free within 12 years using the same income they have now—saving hundreds of thousands for retirement and without having any negative impact on your credit rating.

Chapter 1 provides insight into the economy's financial crisis, soaring debt, the Credit Card Accountability Responsibility and Disclosure Act, increased interest rates, the effects of cash withdrawals, creditors applying payments, different debt types, and the secrets of your credit score.

Chapter 2 discusses taking control of your financial life by creating a financial plan and budget and executing the plan.

Chapter 3 explains the negative impact of doing nothing at all and provides an overview of the debt reduction and elimination options available—an accelerated debt elimination plan, debt consolidation loans, credit card hardship plans offered directly from creditors, professional consumer credit counseling agencies, professional debt settlement, bankruptcy, and do-it-yourself plans.

Chapter 4 discusses the controversy and criticism of the debt settlement industry by reviewing the scams and deceit practiced by some professional debt settlement companies.

Chapter 5 provides an overview of collection agencies and their practices. It also offers insight to the reader on how to handle collection correspondence and how to control the phone conversation.

Chapter 6 provides an in-depth overview of how to successfully negotiate your credit card hardship utilizing a balance liquidation plan that will reduce your interest rates and establish a fixed payment plan, getting you out of debt within 60 months.

Chapter 7 offers a complete overview of do-it-yourself (DIY) debt settlement, explaining why most DIY plans fail and providing you with step-by-step instructions on how you can effectively set yourself up for success and negotiate with your creditor to reduce your debt by 25% to 75%.

Chapter 8 discusses the importance of generating a second income.

Chapter 9 covers how to choose a strategy for eliminating your financial troubles. This chapter recaps pros and cons to help you determine the best program for your financial success.

Chapter 10 discusses symptoms associated with being in debt, such as depression, stress, and anxiety.

Chapter 11 discusses legal proceedings, such as lawsuits and judgments of wage garnishments and liens, and the actions you can take to combat them.

Chapter 12 explains the five key elements of rebuilding your credit score.

Chapter 13 builds upon Chapter 12 by discussing how to research your debts. It explains the statute of limitations and what you need to look for when going over your credit reports. This is a key role in rebuilding your credit.

Chapter 14 provides invaluable information on the statute of limitations on all types of accounts, collection agencies licensing, and bonding requirements, as well as bad-check laws in each state.

Chapter 15 discusses payday loan and explains why you should avoid these types of loans.

Chapter 16 aims to inspire and motivate you to get out of debt by showing the impact debt settlement can have when done correctly. This chapter presents several debt settlement success stories that were negotiated using our do-it-yourself debt settlement model outlined in Chapter 7.

CONTENTS

DIG YOURSELF
OUT OF DEBT

NOTICE OF DISCLAIMER

The information in this book is not intended to be legal advice. All information in this book is for educational purposes only. The information in this book is an accumulation of our years of work knowledge and research in the finance, credit, collection, and debt negotiation industries. Should you have questions or concerns about the integrity of this information—please refer to the source of information, if referenced in this book, and/or research elsewhere and/or contact an attorney for assistance.

CHAPTER 1

UNDERSTANDING CREDIT CARD DEBT AND THE EFFECT OF INTEREST RATES

SOARING DEBT

In 2004 consumer debt was soaring to record levels—the average family had $80,000 in debt, double that from 2003. Some economists were worried that the high personal debt could stall the economy. However, the top economist at the time, Alan Greenspan, was not concerned, as the real-estate market was good and homeowners had plenty of equity in their homes—even though credit card delinquencies, mortgage foreclosures, and bankruptcies were at an all-time high. *(Source: USA Today, 2/23/2004)*

In 2005, due to the increase in bankruptcy filings, Congress enacted new bankruptcy laws, making it difficult for consumers to file bankruptcy. Hence the popularity and rise of the finance industry, specifically credit counseling, debt management, and debt settlement.

By 2008, consumer borrowing in America was at an all-time high, as were consumer debt delinquencies. Credit card delinquencies increased 26% from 2007 to 2008. The average U.S. household owed mortgage or rent payments, student loans, and automobile loans, and had significant credit card debt.

CURRENT ECONOMIC CRISIS

The financial crisis of 2007 to present is a crisis triggered by a liquidity crisis in the U.S. banking system. It has resulted in the collapse of large financial institutions, the bailout of banks by national governments, and downturns in stock markets around the world. In many areas, the housing market has also suffered, resulting in numerous evictions, foreclosures, and prolonged vacancies. It is considered by many economists to be the worst financial crisis since the Great Depression of the 1930s. It has contributed to the failure of key businesses, declines in consumer wealth estimated in the trillions of U.S. dollars, substantial financial commitments incurred by governments, and a significant decline in economic activity. Many causes have been proposed, with varying weight assigned by experts. Both market-based and regulatory solutions have been implemented or are under consideration.

The collapse of a global housing bubble, which peaked in the U.S. in 2006, caused the values of securities tied to real estate pricing to plummet thereafter, damaging financial institutions globally. Questions regarding bank solvency, declines in credit availability, and damaged investor confidence had an impact on global stock markets, where securities suffered large losses during late 2008 and early 2009. Economies worldwide slowed during this period as credit tightened and international trade declined. Critics argued that credit-rating agencies and investors failed to accurately price the risk involved with mortgage-related financial products, and that governments did not adjust their regulatory practices to address current financial markets. Governments and central banks responded with unprecedented fiscal stimulus, monetary policy expansion, and institutional bailouts.

INCREASED INTEREST RATES

Now interest rates on mortgages, credit cards, and other types of consumer loans were set to go higher.

We're not talking about a temporary spike in rates. Rather, economists, who don't often agree on many things, almost all agree that the age of easy credit, which American consumers have enjoyed for the past several decades, is drawing to an end.

It's hard to imagine that 30 years ago, 30-year mortgage rates stood at 18.2%, more than five times higher than the current rates, which now are just above 3.6%.

Since 1981, interest rates have been steadily declining, fueling a partly credit-driven economic boon. Buoyed by easy and cheap credit, American consumers have enjoyed increasingly affluent lifestyles with only modest increases in income. Now, according to economists, the time has come to pay the piper. The combination of high deficits, our nation's burgeoning debt, a weak economy, a weaker dollar, and renewed fears of inflation have all combined to push interest rates higher even as the Fed Funds rate has held mostly steady at record lows for more than a year.

In 2010 mortgage rates were among the first type of consumer loan to show signs of increase, with the rates on 30-year mortgages reaching 5.31%, the highest level in 8 months. Credit card interest rates were steadily on the rise too, in part spurred by the continuing weak economy. According to the Federal Reserve, the average credit card interest rate reached 14.26% in 2010, up from 12.03% in 2008. For the average American household, that 2.23% jump amounts to approximately $200 more down the drain in interest per year. Economists anticipate that credit card rates will increase again at an increased pace, and they expect to see the average credit card APR of 16% to 17%.

As you can see, the access to cheap credit over the past three decades has left many consumers in a vulnerable position financially. While the disposable income increased modestly, from 10.7% to 12.6% over the last 30 years, total household loans increased tenfold, partly fueled by the low interest rates. With interest rates set to go higher, many American consumers will be faced with the harsh reality that, going forward, it will be increasingly expensive to spend more than you earn.

As rates on car loans, mortgages, and credit cards begin to rise, consumers will be forced to cut back on their borrowing. In 2010, household debt was hovering around $13.5 trillion, surpassing the disposable income by $2.55 trillion. Fewer American consumers were able to afford such sizable obligations and households were forced to rely on their income, not credit, to cover expenses.

This turn of events was expected to steer many households into more economically stable positions. Unfortunately, the unwinding of excessive debt levels has not been a smooth process and has left many facing a more severe financial crisis.

Consumer debt continued to rise in 2009 and 2010; credit card companies were taking advantage of many consumers with high interest rates on existing accounts and increasing minimum payment requirements. Many credit card holders received letters advising them that their interest rates have increased. While, other cardholders received notices that their credit limits had been decreased and monthly minimum payments were increased. This is common practice by many creditors for accounts that are near the maximum credit limit. The reason creditor's do this is to mitigate their losses for the risks they take. The end result for credit card companies is greater pretax profits, while the end result for consumers is an increase in their credit-to-debt utilization and debt that is now more difficult to manage. Being unable to meet the increased debt, many consumers were facing going delinquent or had already gone delinquent, and were seeking a resolution to their financial crisis.

TYPE OF DEBT

Generally, there are two types of debt: secured and unsecured. Mortgages, home equity lines, and automobile loans are all examples of secured debt. Credit cards, department store cards, unsecured credit lines, automobile repossessions, and balance due after short sales are all examples of unsecured debt.

HOW CREDITORS APPLY PAYMENTS

Most credit cards operate with a negative order of payment. This means that those with the highest interest rates will be the very last to be paid. However, with the Credit Card Act of 2009, any payment made that is greater than the monthly minimum required payment must be applied to the highest interest rate.

THE NEGATIVE IMPACT OF CASH WITHDRAWALS

Cash withdrawals will hit your wallet extremely hard. That's why you should never do it unless it's an absolute emergency. If you take a cash advance you are likely to be penalized in four different ways, as follows:

➤ Higher interest rate, generally 24.9% or higher.

➤ No grace period. This means that you will start being charged interest as soon as the cash leaves the machine.

➤ Cash withdrawals carry a fee associated with them of 2% to 3%.

➤ Debt from cash withdrawals will remain on your card until you pay all other debt off, meaning you will pay this high interest rate the longest.

CREDIT CARD ACT OF 2009

Officially named the Credit Card Accountability Responsibility and Disclosure Act of 2009, it was signed into law by President Obama in May 2009 (though it did not take effect until February 2010). The act calls for new consumer protections regarding credit cards. Here are the primary changes you should have seen with the new credit card rules:

➢ Time to pay your bill is 21 days instead of 14.

➢ The payment date is the same date each month instead of a floating date.

➢ Card issuers can no longer change annual percentage rate (APR), fees, or finance charges on outstanding balances, unless the rate you were give was an introductory rate (lasting for only a specific amount of time) or your rate was reduced during a short-term hardship arrangement.

➢ If there are any changes in your billing/finance charges, the creditors must notify you 45 days prior to the change taking effect instead of 15 days. And you have the right to opt out.

➢ The creditor must post how long it will take you to get out of debt if you pay the minimum payment due.

➢ Fees for going over the credit card limit are no longer allowed, unless you specifically authorized the credit card company to allow you to make purchases that put you over the limit.

➢ Credit card companies can no longer charge a fee for payment sent by mail, electronically, or via phone, unless you need the payment to be expedited to make the payment due date.

➢ Any payment made that is over the minimum required payment must be applied towards the balance with the highest interest rate.

➢ Credit card companies are not allowed to issue cards to consumers under the age of 21, unless they can prove they have the financial means to repay the debt or they have a cosigner.

The Legislation:

"Credit cards are a fact of life for most middle-class consumers, but companies profit from

*unfair fees and excessive interest rates that keep consumers in debt. With the current credit squeeze, card companies are resorting to these tactics even more frequently. The **Credit Card Accountability, Responsibility, and Disclosure Act** expands consumer protections for people using credit cards. The legislation bans double-cycle billing, a practice card companies use to charge interest on debts that have already been paid on time, and universal default, which increases the interest rate on a credit card based on information unrelated to that card (for example, whether a consumer has paid other bills on time). The Act prohibits retroactive application of interest rate increases, restricts certain fees, and prohibits interest from being charged on fees. When consumers have more than one card balance, card payments must be applied first to the balance with the highest interest rate. The legislation limits over-the-limit fees, fees applied when a cardholder charges more than their credit limit, to one per violation and permits cardholders to prevent transactions that would result in an over-the-limit charge. The Credit Card Accountability, Responsibility, and Disclosure Act expands the information that card companies must provide to consumers, including improved disclosure of due dates and late payment penalties, notice of interest rate increases 45 days before the increase, and the period of time it would take to pay off a card balance if only minimum monthly payments are made. Rules for issuing credit cards to people under 21 are included, along with clarification of rules for on-time bill payment. Finally, the Act enhances the collection of information about credit card billing practices and restricts the use of consumer information by creditors."*
(Source: http://www.gpo.gov/fdsys/pkg/PLAW-111publ24/pdf/PLAW-111publ24.pdf)

SECRETS OF YOUR CREDIT SCORE

Your credit is scored using a complicated formula, but it breaks down into five basic elements: bill paying history, utilization, length of credit history, new credit, and variety of credit.

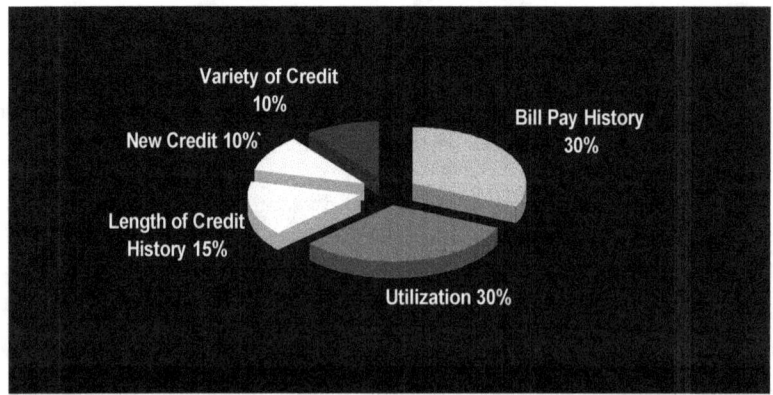

First, do you pay your bills on time? Being late with your payment is very bad for your credit score. How much debt do you actually have and what are the balances you owe? What has your credit history length been? For example, if you have a 30-year mortgage and you have paid it on time for 30 years, that's great for your credit. Do you have new credit? If you do, that hurts your credit score, and a lot of new credit *really* hurts it. Finally, the variety of credit affects your credit score. For example, it's not a good idea to have all credit card debt, which suggests that you are trying to extend your lifestyle with credit cards. But if you have a mortgage, car payment, student loans, and some credit cards, that shows a healthier credit mix.

Mortgage modifications will lower your credit score temporarily because the lender reports the modification to the credit bureaus. However, this is much better than letting your house go into foreclosure. A foreclosure is very bad for your credit score and stays on your credit for 7 years. So, when faced with this decision, modify your mortgage and take the temporary drop in your credit score.

Closing a credit card can also hurt your credit score. That is because it affects credit utilization and how much credit has been extended to you and how much you are using. If you are using a lot of the credit that has been extended, it will lower your score; if you are using very little, your score will remain high. When you close a credit card it lowers your overall extended credit and increases your usage, which lowers your credit score. Congress is now looking into this practice, but has not made any changes to date.

Unpaid library book fines, parking tickets, and traffic fines may have a negative impact on your credit too. More municipalities are sending these fines to collection agencies, which report to the credit bureaus. In addition, unpaid taxes are very bad for your credit score, as tax liens remain on your credit bureau for 7 years.

IMPROVING YOUR CREDIT SCORE

There are three major credit bureaus—Experian, TransUnion, and Equifax—that collect the information that makes up your credit history. This information is used to formulate your credit score. You can improve your credit score through the following steps:

> **Pay your bills on time to start building a good credit history.** Paying on time for a few months can improve your score significantly. Make a budget, cutting out any unnecessary spending, and use the extra cash to get current on overdue bills.

➢ **Pay down credit card debt.** You can improve your credit utilization rate by paying down credit cards and other lines of credit now, starting with any that are maxed out. It may sound obvious, but if you want to improve your credit score, charging more is not recommended.

➢ **Keep lines of credit and try to increase your limits if possible.** Just because you don't want to use your cards doesn't mean you should close the accounts. If self-control is an issue, cut up the cards, but leave the accounts open. Closing cards will shorten your credit history and affect your credit-to-debt utilization, thus hurting your credit score.

Fair Isaac Corporation (FICO) attracts scores up to 850, and ChoicePoint attracts scores up to 997. For both FICO and ChoicePoint, the higher your score, the better your credit rating. The charts below show the breakdowns for credit scores

FICO Score		Choice Point	
Credit Score	**Credit Rating**	**Credit Score**	**Credit Rating**
750-850	Excellent	776-997	Good
660-749	Good	626-775	Average
620-659	Fair	501-625	Below Average
350-619	Poor	Less than 500	Less Desirable

Credit Bureaus

Experian:	TransUnion:	Equifax:
901 West Bond	2 Baldwin Place	PO Box 740256
Lincoln, NE 68521	PO Box 2000	Atlanta, GA 30374
www.experian.com	Chester, PA 19022	www.equifax.com
	www.transunion.com	

Websites

www.annualcreditreport.com Request a free annual credit report	www.bankrate.com Information on credit cards and credit calculators	www.credit.com Comparison of credit card interest rates information, tips, and more

Government Resources

Federal Reserve Board www.federalreserve.gov/pubs/shop/#aprs Information from the federal reserve board on how to understand and compare credit cards and your rights while using a credit card	Federal Trade Commission www.ftc.gov Information on loans, co-signing, credit cards, and debt and credit card trans-fers

CHAPTER 2

TAKING CONTROL OF YOUR FINANCIAL LIFE

CONTROL YOUR MONEY

No matter how much money a family has, they would probably like or need more. However, more money isn't always the answer to financial concerns. Better money management can often help families feel more satisfied with their financial situation. Everyone knows that we sometimes don't think about the money we spend daily. Money leaves our pocket, wallet, or purse and we simply don't remember or register what happened to it. The average American household with credit card debt is $15,900 in debt. *(Source: The Survey of Consumer Payment Choice, Federal Reserve Bank of Boston, 1/2010)*

When you stopped for coffee this morning, how much did you spend for a latte, muffin, tax, and tip? Once you begin to keep track of your spending by writing everything down, then you can take a look at where your money goes and start making better spending decisions.

That's why one of the most important steps in taking control of your financial life is to start writing down what your family actually spends money on each month. This means ***writing down every penny spent***, every single day for a month. Once you have done that, you will be able to make significantly better decisions on what is or is not important to buy, and where you can begin to save money.

Here are five simple steps that will assist you in managing your personal finances:

1. Set short-term and long-term goals.

2. Create a budget and list all your bills and daily expenditures.

3. Create a financial plan for spending and savings, to build financial security.

4. Avoid excessive consumption.

5. Reevaluate spending and savings as conditions change.

Each expense can be entered into a simplified accounting package with or without a computer. If using a computer we recommend setting up an account with one of the following secured sites:

➢ www.mint.com

➢ www.gosimplifi.com

These sites will assist you in your financial planning and give you the ability to create many different reports, which will help you track your expenses and aid in your ongoing planning.

UNDERSTANDING AND CONTROLLING YOUR SPENDING

When you are spending based on a plan, it will reduce or eliminate money concerns and help meet your financial needs.

Your plan of action should show your projected income and expenditures, as well as identify your goals, build financial security, and avoid spending too much on things you may consider unnecessary or unimportant after reviewing them. Remember, your plan is a work in progress; you have to continually go over the plan and look for possible ways to increase income or decrease your expenditures, to meet your financial goals.

You also have to consider and plan for protecting your assets to avoid their misuse and make use of insurance to guard against the risk of loss. There are several different trust/insurances, such as revocable living trust, credit shelter trust, disclaimer trust, and life insurance trust. Consider that you can also increase your total real income by using your time, ability, and materials on hand instead of money whenever possible. By continuing to evaluate, make necessary changes, and follow the plan, your family will be better able to get the most from its money and take charge of how to spend its resources.

PLAN REQUIREMENTS

No one can tell you how to use your money or what your lifestyle should be. It's your job to make a plan for managing your income. However, generally, we recommend following this breakdown:

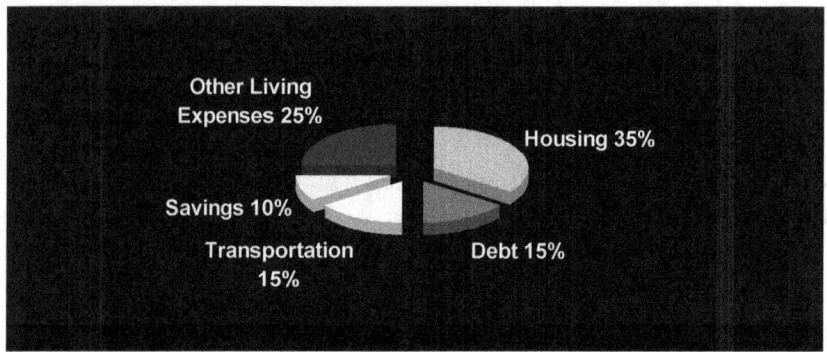

Housing: Your mortgage/rent, maintenance, taxes, utilities, and insurance. Simply, the cost of your dwelling and the actual costs to live there.

Debt: Credit cards, student loans, personal loans/line of credit, and any debt that you owe over and above any mortgage and automobile loans.

Transportation: Car payments, insurance, and repairs, as well as gas, tolls, and parking, bus, and train expenses.

Savings: All money you are putting away for your emergency fund, retirement, college fund, and other savings and goals.

Other Living Expenses: Additional expenses, such as groceries, dining out, vacations, entertainment, clothing, gifts, health care, and all other items you spend your money on daily.

If you use this plan as a family plan, everyone has to work as a team. You'll need to talk with each other all the time so that individual differences and common goals can be identified. Each member must then practice money control in order to stick to the plan. If one person doesn't follow the plan, everyone will suffer.

One suggestion is to set aside an allowance for each person to use for personal expenses (even including children as young as 5 or 6 years old). Individuals do not have to account for how they spend their allowance, which may eliminate some conflicts and avoid disputes over small amounts.

Keep your record-keeping simple so that it does not feel like a burden. You might appoint the family member who enjoys organizing the most to keep the records, but everyone has the responsibility to know what records to keep track of, and where the complete set of family records can be found at all times.

SET REALISTIC GOALS

Did you know there are actually three types of money?

1. **Money income** is the actual income in dollars and cents.

2. **Real income** is the total goods and services that income will buy. If you are careful and smart, you can use sound buying habits to achieve greater real income from your money income.

3. **Psychological income**, on the other hand, is the amount of satisfaction one receives from purchased goods and services. Ultimately, psychological income (satisfaction) is the most important. You only get this type of satisfaction when you set goals and manage your money to meet those goals.

Your goal is to get the most satisfaction (psychological income) possible. You can do this by setting spending priorities (real income) based on your long-term and short-term goals. That way, when you spend your actual income (money income) you will be spending it on things you need and want to save for. Think about where your family is today and where it wants to be in 5 to 10 years. You have to plan to attain these dreams. Spend your money on making these dreams come true.

It is extremely important to write down very specific and very realistic goals. As circumstances change, and as individuals and the family go through various stages of their lives, the family's goals, timetable, and spending plan will need to be updated. Because every individual decision impacts your ability to meet your goals, the whole family should be a part of the budgeting process. We suggest that you schedule a regular time for a family discussion about budgeting.

The objective of the plan is to help your family reach its goals, not to make them follow strict rules. Don't get discouraged if the first plan doesn't work.

Keep reworking the plan to fit your family's changing needs and desires. Arrange a set period to revisit the plan to see if it's working.

Long-term goals and objectives can give overall direction to your financial planning. These goals are usually set for 5 to 10 years into the future. Stock investments, college funds, and a down payment on a house are examples of long-term goals.

Keep in mind that many factors will influence these plans. Be willing to be flexible and make adjustments as needed. Intermediate goals should be obtainable within 1 to 3 years. A dream vacation or a new kitchen may be intermediate goals. Short-term goals are those attainable in the next 3 months to one year, such as buying a new appliance or winter coats.

Both intermediate and short-term goals are often part of a long-term goal. For example, a long-term goal of saving for a college education may be broken down into annual goals of saving $500 for each child in a college fund. When writing your intermediate and short-term goals be very specific about time periods and dollar amounts so that you can easily measure your progress in achieving your long-term goal. (Use the worksheet in the appendix to record your goals.)

GETTING STARTED ON A BUDGET

Step 1. Decide how you will keep copies of your receipts. Here are some methods:

- **Receipt Method:** All family members save receipts from all purchases. A container for receipts is placed where it is easily accessible to all members—for example, on the refrigerator. Receipts are totaled on a regular basis, typically weekly.

- **Envelope Method:** This cash system allows each family member to see how much money is available in a budget category or each envelope. It requires very little paperwork since expenditures are simply recorded on the envelope. Receipts can also be kept in the envelope. One disadvantage of this system is that it does require keeping larger amounts of cash around the house, which could become a security problem.

- **Checkbook Method:** This is a record-keeping method where each expense is paid by check and recorded immediately, and the balance is kept up to date. Many families choose this type of system. Investigate the many types of checking accounts available to best meet your needs. This method is most compatible with some computer programs or online services.

- **Account Method:** This is the method preferred those who want to keep a detailed daily record. Usually the record-keeping task is assigned to one family member, but all family members should understand the system and help keep receipts. This method also assists in keeping accurate records for tax purposes.

Step 2. Decide what time frame the budget should cover:

- Most families develop an annual budget to plan income and expenses, plus guidelines for monthly spending. Using a set time period will make record-keeping an easier habit to develop. We recommend you keep track of income and expenses for at least 6 months.

Step 3. Decide how you will track your income and expenses; there are several options to you can use:

- The Expense Planning Worksheet (located in the appendix).

- An online secure online service, such as

    o www.mint.com

    o www.gosimplifi.com

- A computer record-keeping systems, such as QuickBooks® or Money.

- A spreadsheet that you design yourself.

- A check register to track spending.

For most people the simplest way to do record-keeping is to list earnings and expenditures when money is actually received or paid out.

Note: One advantage of keeping computer-based records instead of handwritten records is that data can be stored and retrieved almost instantaneously. Records can then be printed out quickly and comparisons can be easily calculated.

Step 4. Tracking your expenses.

In the appendix, you will find the Expense/Spending Worksheet. Please fill it out as best you can. Make copies and add your expenditures to them. Write down your estimates of what you spend each week. Then, keep track of *all* your expenses for at least 3 months. Moreover, make sure you account for every penny you spend. You will be surprised at the difference between what you think you spend and what you actually spend.

Most people don't like doing this because the reality of what they spend can be a shock. But, if you're going to change your overall debt, you will need to make some spending changes. This worksheet will help you identify where you can save each week, month, and year.

Each member of the family should have a dollar amount set aside for their own personal use (haircuts, clothing, movies, dining out, mobile phone, dry cleaning, spending money, etc.).

Step 5. Forecasting your family's income.

On the Income Plan Worksheet in the appendix, list all the cash your family expects to receive for the next year and then for the next 5 years. If the income is from wages or salary, include only take-home pay. If it is from a business, farm, or trade, make the best possible estimate. Add other cash income, such as interest or dividends from investments, pensions, annuities, veterans benefits, life insurance proceeds, and rents.

Step 6. Setting your family's goals.

Now you know what family's spending habits and income. Next you're ready to estimate how much money will be needed for the goals the family has set and when it will be needed. A long-term goal might be a college fund for a child; an intermediate goal might be to start a savings account; and a short-term goal might be to reduce expenses by not dining out for 2 years. See the appendix for a Goals Worksheet.

Step 7. Revise your spending and income worksheets so that you can meet your goals.

Based on your goals, use the Revised Expense/Spending Worksheet found in the appendix to revise your spending plan and then track what you actually spend.

Step 8. Re-forecast your family's income.

On the Revised Income Plan Worksheet found in the appendix, revise any income your family expects to receive for the next year and then for the next 5 years.

Step 9. Review your goals, expenses, and income until you get a match.

> ➢ Now, do you have enough money each month to pay your everyday living expenses and save for your goals?

16

> If not, can income be increased or must some goals be eliminated?

  o How can you increase your income?

  o Which goals could you eliminate or modify? Rank goals in order of importance to determine which to eliminate.

If the spending total is greater than income, make adjustments in "other living expenses," but don't readjust by immediately slashing out one entire classification completely. Here are a few suggestions:

> Don't cut food expenses drastically. They may seem high, but cut too much and the plan will be impossible to follow. Instead, reduce dining out and/or entertainment expenses.

> Don't expect to know the exact spending limits for each category until you have tracked your spending for a few months.

> Don't downgrade personal allowances. They may be small and seem insignificant, but they're very important.

> Do make reasonable deposits to your savings before paying any other expenses. Savings are a significant part of your plan, either for an emergency fund or for goals.

> Do leave room for unexpected expenses; everyone has them from time to time. But don't get discouraged! Millions of people are forced to juggle their spending so they have enough left to finance the expenses they consider essential or most desirable. The longer you are on the plan, the easier it will become to follow and to adjust.

Step 10. Keep track of your expenses monthly and income for the year.

Now, track your actual expenses during the year. Then, take the figures from the Monthly Expense/Spending Worksheets and your Monthly Income Plan Worksheet, and enter those numbers on the Income and Expenses Worksheet for the Year Worksheet found in the appendix. Remember, each member of the family should have a set amount of money for personal use.

Step 11. Continue to evaluate your family's spending.

Evaluating your family budget allows you to compare the actual amounts with the planned amounts to see where you are in the budgeting process. The more frequently you make such checks, the better the overview of your progress in reaching both long-term and short-term goals will be. Making necessary adjustments will make your goals more realistic and attainable.

Evaluation is a continual process. No one budget will be perfect. The budgeting process might be referred to as a financial map: you need to determine where you are going (set goals), plan your route (budget), and make adjustments along the way (evaluate).

Step 12. Complete your Balance Sheet Worksheet.

Each year at tax time, it is a good idea to review all your assets and liabilities. In the appendix, you'll find a Balance Sheet Worksheet. Fill out the Assets side of the Balance Sheet Worksheet. The value of home furnishings, land, automobiles, etc., will be based on what those assets are actually worth today in cash. Don't overestimate the value of your assets.

Next, fill out the Liabilities side of the Balance Sheet. List exactly what you owe. For example, how much alimony do you have to pay each year? How much in automobile payments will you spend during the year? Don't forget property taxes. These are large categories that occur every year.

EFFECTIVE PLANNING

In order for your budget to work well, it must be realistic. This means you must be practical when you estimate both income and expenses, realizing that there are often conflicting needs and wants within the family, and that external factors can affect your budget. The following suggestions can help in getting the most for your family's money:

> ➢ Develop a family system for handling money that involves everyone's cooperation.

> ➢ Be realistic about needs, demands, and what the family can afford. Plan and purchase basic essentials first.

> ➢ Establish a habit of planning ahead for long-term and short-term goals. Be prepared to take advantage of special sale prices on planned purchases when they do occur (a savings of 25% or more may be realized).

> ➢ Become informed about the retail market situation, availability, and prices of products, including seasonal values.

> ➢ Practice sound shopping habits and try to get the best buy; always "buy," never "be sold" items. Make a habit of doing pre-shopping research. For example, warehouse stores may offer value but require you to buy much greater quantities than you can use, thereby negating any savings.

➢ Use and care for goods to get the maximum service with a minimum of repairs and maintenance costs.

➢ Use your own ability, talent, and time to perform as many services as possible at home rather than buying these services.

➢ Use credit wisely and keep credit costs to a minimum.

➢ Keep accurate records and avoid overpayment of income taxes.

➢ Don't become addicted to designer labels, prestige stores, specialty shops, and store gimmicks. Evaluate the quality of product as well as its price.

➢ Take advantage of public parks, libraries, and services and use them when possible.

➢ Be alert to fraud, and exercise consumer rights and responsibilities in the selection, purchase, and use of goods and services. It is estimated that the average consumer loses 5% of their income due to unwise consumer habits.

➢ Study the habits of family members. Identify and eliminate waste, such as buying convenience or luxury items or overbuying in quantities. Avoid spending on impulse, misusing goods, and discarding useful items. Keep accurate records of how money is used. Periodically, maybe quarterly, evaluate your progress in using money, and then make adjustments.

Putting together a financial plan can be a bit scary, especially if it's your first time. But you don't have to go it alone. We recommend that you visit www.gosimplfi.com or www.mint.com.

A GUIDE TO FINANCIAL TERMS

Assets can be broken down into three basic categories:

➢ **Monetary assets:** Cash and items that can be readily converted to cash and used for living expenses or savings and emergencies.

➢ **Tangible assets:** Physical items primarily used to maintain lifestyle, but could be sold to raise cash—for example, your car, furniture, or exercise equipment.

> **Investment assets:** Tangible or intangible items obtained for producing additional income, or held for speculated increase in value.

Balance sheet: A financial snapshot; an overview of an individual's or family's financial condition at a given time. It's also known as a statement of financial position or position statement; it summarizes the assets and liabilities of a business entity at a certain time.

Budget or spending plan: A reckoning of the amounts expected to be received or spent within a specific time. Revising such estimates is necessary periodically. When budgeted expenses exceed budgeted income, three alternatives are recommended:

> earn more income,

> cut back expenses, or

> a combination of the two.

Cash flow calendar: Estimations of the annual income and expenses for each budget time period are recorded on this sheet to help determine surplus or deficit situations. Effective management of cash flow can include reducing expenses during months with financial deficits, increasing income, using planned savings, using emergency savings, or borrowing.

Comparison shopping: Simply using an informed process of comparing products or services to find those that best fit your budget and needs.

Consumer price index: Published monthly by the U.S. Bureau of Labor Statistics, this index provides a broad measure of the cost of living for consumers. The index represents a statistical average of prices expressed as a percentage of a base period. Basically, it shows whether prices for a particular item, such as food or clothing, have risen or fallen since the last comparison period. However, a number of specific price indexes are compiled privately.

Expenses can be broken down into categories:

> **Fixed expenses:** Expenditures usually of the same amount for each budgeted time period, such as rent, car payments, loan installments, and regular savings.

> **Variable expenses:** Expenditures that may fluctuate due to individual control, such as groceries, dining out, utilities, and furnishings. Variable expenses are the easiest ones to juggle in times of financial difficulty.

Financial planning: A coordinated series of plans, beginning with goals and objectives that reflect your values, attitudes, lifestyle circumstances, wants, and needs. This process helps you to develop and implement financial moves to reach financial objectives.

Financial skills: The techniques of decision-making in personal financial management, such as budget preparation, record-keeping, savings, and investment plan and use of credit.

Financial statement: A summary of individual or family finances on an annual or other basis.

Net income: Income after taxes, the total amount available for individual or family expenses.

Net-worth statement: A statement showing the difference between total assets and total liabilities for an individual or a family.

Personal spending style: How you spend money, influenced by your values, emotions, attitudes, and other factors resulting from life experiences. Conflict of spending styles may result in disagreement over family finances.

Pre-shopping research: Gathering information on products before a final selection is made.

Real income: Income that is measured in constant prices relative to some base time period.

Spending plan: A plan for spending and saving family resources to meet identified goals—that is, a budget.

Negotiating with retailers: It is always a good idea to try to negotiate a price with your retailer. Consider these shopping statistics:

> - 72.4% of shoppers have tried negotiating prices with retailers. *(Source: America's Research Group, 3/2009)*
>   - In 1999, only 32% of the shoppers surveyed said that they negotiated with retailers over pricing.
> - 94% of shoppers said that they were successful when negotiating a price on furniture at least once over the past 3 years. *(Source: Consumer Reports, 11/2007.)* People have negotiated for:
>   - Floor and demo models: 65%
>   - Furniture: 49%

- o   Large and small appliances: 39%

- o   Jewelry: 38%

- o   Home electronics: 35%

SEVEN MONEY MISTAKES WE MAKE EVERY DAY

These money mistakes may not seem to cost us much, but even small errors, multiplied over a lifetime, can add up to a small fortune.

In the hope of making better financial decisions, review this list of common money mistakes:

1. **Buying expensive mutual funds**. Do you know how much you pay for the mutual funds in your retirement account? If you don't know, you're not alone. Mutual fund companies don't send out monthly or quarterly bills. Instead, they quietly deduct their fees from the returns on your investments. These fees, quoted as an expense ratio (a 1% fee means you're paying 1% of your account balance in fees each year), add up to thousands of dollars over a lifetime of investing. To see how much you are paying, track the actual expense of your mutual funds and ETFs (exchange traded funds), which this is an investment fund traded on stock exchanges, much like stocks. You can track your portfolio on Morningstar, including the total cost of your investments.

2. **Neglecting credit scores.** Credit scores have a major impact on our financial lives. An excellent credit score results in lower interest rates on mortgages, car loans, and credit cards. It also results in lower insurance premiums. However, many do not know their credit score or how their financial decisions shape their score. The first step is to regularly review your credit report, which is available free from www.annualcreditreport.com. You can get a free report from each of the three major credit bureaus once a year. Checking each report for errors can not only improve your credit score, but also help guard against identity theft. While your report will not include your credit score, there are several options to do so.

3. **Equating monthly payments with affordability.** Far too many of us decide whether we can afford something based on whether we can manage the monthly payment. This is particularly true for homes, cars, and furniture. Just because we can handle a payment does not mean we can truly afford something. Monthly payments also ignore

the true cost of ownership. A car, for example, costs a lot more than the monthly payment when you consider insurance, gas, repairs, and maintenance. Instead of focusing on the monthly payment, separate needs from wants and evaluate how you might better use the money. If you still have consumer debt, for example, consider paying the debt off before buying something that will commit you to future monthly payments potentially for years to come.

4. **Overpaying on a mortgage.** Reducing your mortgage by 1% can result in substantial savings. Whether because of falling mortgage rates, which are at historic lows, or an improved credit score, many people may be able to save thousands of dollars over the life of their home loan by refinancing. Yet, for various reasons, many have not taken advantage of falling rates. Even if you have a low rate now, see if you can do better. In some cases, a savings of just 1% or less can justify the cost of refinancing.

5. **Missing good deals online.** Thanks to the Internet, you can find deals, coupons, and promo codes on just about anything. And many retailers offer additional discounts if you buy online. From cell phones to home improvement, the savings can be substantial, and shopping online is often far more convenient than driving around town and waiting in lines. The problem is that we often make purchases completely unaware that these deals exist. To find these bargains, search online for coupons before you make significant purchases and bookmark coupon sites such as www.retailmenot.com and www.fatwallet.com, which regularly update the latest offers from popular retailers.

6. **Overpaying taxes.** A big tax refund can be a source of much-needed cash each year. But a tax refund is the result of having too much tax withheld from your paycheck, which gives the government an interest-free loan with your money. Instead of letting the government hold on to your money for up to a year, adjust your withholdings so you can pocket your money now. The goal should be to match your withholdings as close as possible to your tax liability.

7. **Making minimum payments on credit cards.** Even low-interest credit cards charge a high interest rate. As a result, making the minimum payment on credit card debt adds a lot of interest to your total payments over the life of that debt. Making just the minimum payment also extends the time it takes to pay off the debt by many years. Rather than making just the minimum payment, commit to paying more than the minimum, even if by just a few dollars. Reexamine your budget in an effort to increase the payment as much as possible.

Websites that can help you save money:

www.mint.com

Free online money management program.

www.gosimplifi.com

Free online money management program.

www.coupons.com

Print more than 100 coupons per week.

www.couponmom.com

Printable coupons and tips on how to save at the supermarket.

www.grocerygame.com

Get a list of the lowest-priced items at your local supermarket matched with manufacturers' coupons and weekly specials.

www.shortcuts.com

Get coupons automatically sent to your supermarket's store loyalty card.

www.smartsource.com

Printable coupons, online deals, local grocery deals, and grocery circulars.

CHAPTER 3

GET EDUCATED AND KNOW YOUR DEBT OPTIONS

When you are being overwhelmed by credit card debt, you have several options available to you:

1. Do nothing and hope things get better.

2. Enroll in an accelerated debt elimination plan.

3. Practice debt consolidation.

4. Enroll in credit counseling or debt management.

5. Enroll in a debt settlement program.

6. File bankruptcy.

DO NOTHING AND HOPE THINGS GET BETTER

Americans have charged over 1 trillion dollars worth of goods and services on their credit cards. Unfortunately, the average household has over $11,000 in credit card debt. These days it's common for families to have $25,000,

$35,000, and even $75,000 or more of credit card debt. No type of debt destroys a family faster than credit card debt.

When you use credit cards, unless you pay your balances in full each month, you are putting yourself behind the eight ball. Some 78% of American consumers pay only the monthly minimum on their credit cards. Because only the monthly minimum is being paid, each time a charge is made the credit card balance increases and interest is accruing on the new charge as well as the old charges. Your balances continue to grow and your minimum monthly payment increases as well. These increases are rapid, and before you know it, you are struggling to meet the monthly minimum payment.

By the time you get to the point where you are barely able to make your minimums each month you already know you are in trouble. Now many people start to borrow from one card to pay off another card's balance. The next step from here is not being able to meet your obligations, and those low-interest rate cards that seemed so attractive at first will begin to increase their interest rates to well over 20%. Banks also have the ability to increase your interest rates to 38% at their discretion (this is part of the universal default). Unfortunately, most people choose to do nothing by the time they get into this situation. Procrastination can be a very expensive habit when it comes to handling your creditors. Hoping the problem will go away is not a real option. Late fees and increased finance charges will continue to mount, and it will become an overwhelming situation both financially and emotionally. Eventually your debts must be handled.

This may surprise you, but many people are unaware of what it means to pay off their credit card debt. Very often, they either don't understand the time frame and amounts involved, or worse, have unrealistic expectations of how much they actually owe.

The following illustrates a typical series of credit card debt scenarios, along with the total amount required to pay back the debt and the period of time required for the amount to be paid in full. The numbers will probably surprise you!

Total Credit Card Charges	Charges Plus 19% Interest	Number of Years to Repay
$10,000	$26,276.59	42 years 9 months
$15,000	$55,370.41	48 years 11 months
$20,000	$74,464.22	53 years 3 months
$25,000	$93,557.98	56 years 7 months
$30,000	$112,651.77	59 years 4 months
$35,000	$131,745.58	61 years 8 months
$40,000	$150,839.39	63 years 9 months

$45,000	$169,933.22	65 years 6 months
$50,000	$189,027.02	67 years 1 months
$60,000	$227,214.61	69 years 10 months
$70,000	$265,402.22	72 years 2 months
$80,000	$303,589.81	74 years 2 months
$90,000	$341,777.43	76 years
$100,000	$379,965.06	77 years 7 months
$110,000	$418,152.62	79 years
$120,000	$456,340.27	80 years 4 months
$130,000	$494,527.82	81 years 6 months
$140,000	$532,712.48	82 years 8 months
$150,000	$570,903.04	83 years 8 months

Note: Number of years to pay off a credit card balance based on 19% interest and a minimum monthly of 2.1% of the outstanding balance. Most cards require a minimum monthly payment between 2.0% and 2.4% of the outstanding balance. *(Source: CNN Money)*

We are a credit-driven society and most of us use our credit cards daily. But few of us are aware of the consequences associated with our charging habits. The following is a list of the alarming statistics that are associated with living on credit:

➢ The typical credit card purchase is 115% higher than if using cash.

➢ Over 60% of U.S. families spend more than they earn.

➢ The average U.S. household has five credit cards.

➢ The average household has a total credit card balance of approximately $15,900.

➢ Typical minimum monthly payment is 90% interest and only 10% principal.

➢ 78% of all credit card accounts have only the minimum monthly payment amount being made by the consumer.

➢ Americans paid out approximately $69 billion in interest in 2007 alone.

➢ Credit card companies can increase your interest rate as high as 38% (Universal Default Clause).

➢ U.S. consumer debt has topped $2.55 trillion dollars for the first time ever. Consumer debt continues to grow at an alarming rate.

> ➢ 85% of all Americans are three paychecks away from bankruptcy.

ACCELERATED DEBT ELIMINATION PLAN (ADEP)

We are huge advocates of accelerated debt elimination plans (ADEP). We say this even understanding that we are a credit-driven society and one needs the ability to use credit for purchases from time to time, whether it's to buy a house or car or that 60" plasma television. We believe every consumer who has a mortgage, uses a credit card, or has any type of open credit lines secured or unsecured, should implement and utilize an ADEP for money management. Not only will a solid ADEP save you thousands of dollars, it will also help you save, protect, and grow your money. As you can see, ADEP is for everyone—not just for those who are overwhelmed with debt!

Depending on your financial situation, an ADEP may or may not help you. One thing is for certain; if you are current and paying your bills now, a solid ADEP will save you thousands of dollars and best of all no one will know you are doing it and it will not harm your credit—in fact it is likely to improve your credit.

An accelerated payment plan allows you to turn the tables on your credit card companies. These days, with penalty fees, universal interest default, and all kinds of other traps, it can be hard to stay ahead of the credit card companies. An accelerated repayment plan allows you to pay your debts back in the most efficient and least expensive way possible, and because you will have a specific date that you will be debt-free, you're more motivated to succeed.

The beauty of an ADEP is that it's confidential; you don't have to cut up your credit cards, and once you get started, you can create tremendous momentum. As an added bonus, as you start paying off your debt using an accelerated repayment plan, your credit rating may improve. Better credit means lower rates on your debts, and it may even lower your insurance premiums too. That means even more money in your pocket to pay toward your debts.

Here's how it works: Each month you're paying and paying on your debt. And if you're like 78% of the people using credit cards, your balances seem to stay pretty much the same, or maybe even go up instead of down. The good thing about this is you already have the discipline to pay the fixed amount every month. So, using the same income you have now, you can eliminate 30 years worth of debt in as little as 12 years. With your balances paid off, you will have freed up a significant amount of money that you can now turn into wealth and put toward retirement.

HOW ADEP ELIMINATES DEBT

You start paying your credit cards, mortgages, and/or automobile loans bi-weekly instead of monthly. Why? Every year there are 2 months that have five weeks in them; during those months an extra payment will be made (known as your "power payment"). So, if your bills total X per month, this will create an extra X twice each year. You will apply your power payment twice yearly to your creditors that are charging the highest interest rate.

Example: If your bills are $2,500, of which $1,450 is your mortgage, $450 is your car loan, and two credit cards that are $300 each. Your ADEP system will pay all of your bills on time, and when the extra money becomes available, the system will pay the $1,250 ($2,500 divided by 2) twice each year on the highest interest loan, usually a credit card, until it's paid in full. Once the first credit card is paid off, it will take the extra $300 from that card and apply it to the second credit card, plus the extra $1,250 that's available twice each year, until the second credit card is paid in full. After the second card is paid off, the system will take the extra $600 a month (the two credit cards that are paid off at $300 each), plus the $1,250 twice each year, and that total will be paid on your car loan until it's paid in full. From this point forward every year, the system will take the extra $1,050 each month ($600 from the two credit cards, and $450 from the car) plus the $1250 twice each year and pay your mortgage until the balance is zero.

DEBT CONSOLIDATION LOANS

Taking your existing debt and rolling it into a single loan is a good idea in theory, especially with interest rates being as low as they are. However, before you do this, you need to be certain that a consolidation loan makes sense and will fit into your financial plan and budget.

Consumers are tempted by the low interest rates being offered and often take on additional debt to pay off existing debts. The goal is to consolidate higher-interest loans, credit lines, and credit card balances by rolling them into one easier-to-handle and less-costly payment. But be careful of what looks to be a quick fix as there are risks involved!

A debt consolidation loan is not a cure for your debt problems. There are various debt consolidation options, such as balance transfers to a zero percent credit card and a home equity line of credit (HELOC). However, this approach usually doesn't work and can be very dangerous to your financial situation. Seventy percent of American consumers who take out a HELOC or other type of loan to pay off their credit card debt ultimately end up with the same debt load with which they stared, and oftentimes, saddled with more debt within 2 years. That's because when you take on additional debt to pay off existing debt you're following the same tendencies that got you in debt in the first place. By taking on another creditor you are simply adding more debt to your existing debt. Additionally, depending on the amount of debt that you currently have, you may not qualify for the low interest rates you see advertised. Generally, those low-interest rate loans are for consumers with an excellent credit rating.

However, if you are certain that you will be disciplined by cutting—and not using—those credit cards, debt consolidation may be something to consider despite its risks. The following are some popular forms of debt consolidation—how they work and their pros and cons.

HOME EQUITY LINE OF CREDIT (HELOC)

HELOCs are often advertised as a quick and easy way to eliminate your debt. By leveraging your home's value, you can get money to pay off other bills and a tax break, too.

But borrowing against your house can backfire in a very big way. The biggest risk: You could lose your home if you default on the loan. When you get a HELOC, you are taking on unsecured debt and paying it off with secured debt. Failure to pay it back can result in a home foreclosure. Of course, you are not planning to default, but you never know when a hardship could occur and what the severity of that hardship will be.

While equity loan interest generally is tax deductible, it could be limited in some situations. Even when it does provide a tax break, it doesn't mean it makes fiscal sense.

Banks will tell you how much you can borrow, but that doesn't mean you should borrow the total amount. Typically, however, people borrow the maximum that the bank allows them to borrow.

A home equity line of credit or loan to pay off creditors can work for some consumers overwhelmed with the burden of debt. But, be sure to do your homework to ensure that the home equity dollars make sense. We recommend using a debt-reduction calculator to help determine whether borrowing against your home's equity is a wise move. My two favorite calculators can be found at:

> http://www.bankrate.com/calculators/managing-debt/borrowing-calculator.aspx

> http://cgi.money.cnn.com/tools/debtplanner/debtplanner.jsp

15-Year, $50,000 HELOC			
FICO Score	Average APR	Monthly Payments	Total Repayment
750-850	4.455%	$381.09	$68,596.68
660-749	4.518%	$382.96	$68,932.22
620-659	No Rate Available	Not Available	Not Available
350-619	No Rate Available	Not Available	Not Available

APR = Percentage rate; FICO Score = Fair Isaac Corporation Score or your credit score.

(Source: http://www.bankrate.com/funnel/home-equity/?prods=437. New Jersey Rates March 4, 2013; note: HELOC rates vary from state to state.)

ZERO-PERCENT CREDIT CARD

Consumers who do not own a home or who have no equity in their home usually turn to zero-percent credit cards or credit cards with a single-digit interest rate to reduce debt. This "teaser rate" entices consumers to switch credit card companies. Usually, card companies target those consumers with a better credit score, so someone struggling with debt may not get this option.

Even if you do qualify for a zero-percent or similar single-digit rate, the rate will not last forever. Make sure you know when the rate ends and what the rate is expected to jump to when it does.

Remember, these low rates only last if you make your payments on time. One late payment and the credit card company will increase your rate. Also, look out for hidden fees and charges that can increase the actual cost of borrowing.

A zero-percent or single-digit credit card is definitely a short-term fix. The only way it benefits you is if you're meticulous about making your payments on time and you move the debt to another low-interest rate credit card before the rate expires. Beware of opening a new credit card account every 6 months, as this could negatively affect your credit rating. Also, to successfully decrease your debt load, you will need to pay at least double the minimum required monthly payment. For example, if you transfer $20,000 of debt to a zero-percent credit card and pay $1,000 on it by making only the minimum monthly payments, by the time the rate jumps to 14%, it will take you 1,134 months or 94.5 years to erase your remaining $19,000 balance, and you will have paid $64,805 in interest. That's assuming you don't charge another penny during that time.

DEBT CONSOLIDATION LOANS

Debt consolidation loans are very appealing because of their convenience. Instead of paying several different creditors who are charging different rates at different times of the month, you take out one big loan and pay off all those accounts with a single payment once a month. But convenience does not always equal savings.

Before you agree and sign for the loan, be sure that the costs of the new, bundled loan will truly be less than what you're currently paying the various creditors. Many candidates for a consolidation loan do not qualify for the lowest interest rate available because of their low credit score. Plus, when there is nothing to secure the loan (such as a home or car), expect the lender to increase the rate as their risk for recovery is now increased.

Calculate interest and fees on all your existing accounts to determine the total of the payments you now make. Then compare those amounts with the consolidation loan numbers to make sure it truly is a better financial choice. As with any product, shop around for the best rate.

CREDIT CARD DEBT HARDSHIP PROGRAMS

Most credit card companies offer credit card hardship programs for consumers overwhelmed with debt and struggling to make their monthly minimum payments. Last year, almost 3 million American consumers were receiving some type of assistance from these plans. These programs are geared toward helping consumers reduce and eliminate outstanding credit card debt.

Creditors are willing to work with their cardholders in order to be repaid the principal loan amount borrowed rather than seeing the consumer not pay anything, default on the debt, or file for bankruptcy, in which case these credit card companies and banks may receive nothing from you.

While the hardship programs provided vary from creditor to creditor, it is possible to get a temporary or permanent reduction on the interest rate you are paying. Most creditors will offer you a short-term hardship program that will reduce your interest rate or reduce your payment for 6 months to 1 year, with the hope that you will be able to resume your normal monthly payment within that time frame. Some creditors may be able to withhold finance charges from 1 to 5 years.

More and more creditors are trying to provide additional information about their hardship assistance programs offered. Many creditors are mailing cardholders materials about these hardship programs, which include a phone number to call for assistance. If you are in a financial crisis, you do not have to wait to receive something in the mail—simply contact your creditor(s) to let them know you are having financial difficulties in paying the account. Keep in mind that each creditor has their own hardship program and qualifications may vary.

If you are one of the many who have fallen behind on making your credit card payments, then you understand how difficult it can be to catch up on your bills. Your outstanding balance will grow quickly as the numerous fees, penalties, and interest costs accumulate. You need to take advantage of the hardship programs offered by the creditors to reduce your monthly payments. If you are recently delinquent, most creditors will work with you to bring your account to good standing—helping to reduce late fees, over-the-limit fees, and other fees and costs the creditors may be charging you.

The credit card debt assistance and financial hardship programs are designed for consumers who are experiencing a true financial hardship. If you are able to pay your credit card bills and are only looking for a quick, easy way to lower your credit card payments, then these hardship programs are not for you. If you have the income, assets, or resources to pay your creditors in a timely manner, hardship programs are not for you. If you fall into this category, we highly recommend an ADEP as discussed earlier in this chapter.

CREDIT CARD BALANCE LIQUIDATION PLAN (BLP)

Similar to loan workouts, these plans aim to help borrowers avoid a default and help them restructure their credit card debt. It's an agreement between the borrower and the credit card company. Under the agreement, the borrower sets up a payment plan with the credit card company, and the bank then reduces the interest rates and sometimes even lowers your monthly payment to a level you can afford to pay monthly. Some credit card companies call their program by a different name.

BLPs are designed to have you out of debt within 60 months. The creditor will close your account, reduce your interest rate (usually between 4% and 9%), and set you up on a monthly payment schedule. The monthly payment is the same amount each month.

We recommend BLPs over other hardship programs offered by creditors. Why? The main reason that banks offer hardship programs is that they hope that you will get back on a solid financial footing and be able resume making full payments on your account and monthly credit card bills. But with a BLP, once you are back on solid ground financially, you can either continue with your monthly scheduled payments or increase the payments to pay off the balances earlier, instead or reverting back to the higher interest rates. Remember, as with almost all businesses, credit card companies and banks are primarily concerned about making a profit. Therefore, they want to take the 6-month to a year short-term fix instead of a long-term BLP. The short-term offer may sound better at first, but in the end, we believe the BLP is your best option.

CAN MY BALANCE BE REDUCED IN A HARDSHIP PROGRAM?

Yes, your balance can be reduced; if your credit cards become seriously delinquent, creditors will reduce your credit card balance if they see that you are heading toward filing bankruptcy. In most cases, the creditor will eventually agree to a lump-sum settlement plan with you to close out your current account. Learn more about lump-sum settlements later in this chapter.

DISADVANTAGES OF HARDSHIP PLANS

Many banks have rules that make it difficult to apply for a hardship program. Plus, these hardship programs may have some disadvantages associated with them—for example:

- ➢ There is absolutely no guarantee that you will be able to reduce interest rates.

- ➢ You are not guaranteed to have your total outstanding debt reduced.

- ➢ There may be some potential repercussions if you ask for a hardship program, such as a negative impact on your credit score.

- ➢ Most likely, the credit account will be closed.

- ➢ Creditors may "flag" you as a risky customer, which might result in a lower credit limit.

- ➢ Creditors are going to hold you to the terms of your current agreement if they think you can pay, and while they are more open to modifications, they may not negotiate with you.

WHO WON'T A HARDSHIP PROGRAM ASSIST?

Lenders will not offer hardship programs if you show you have the means and ability to repay your loans. A debt-to-income ratio (DIR) above 50% shows a clear economic hardship. However, you must show the creditor that there is a benefit to enrolling you into their hardship program and that you can afford to meet your new payment obligations on a monthly basis long term. Creditors have a very thin line between the maximum and minimum allowed for positive cash flow after all expenses are paid. However, the creditors will not tell you what this range is and it varies from creditor to creditor. They will simply inform you whether you have been accepted into the hardship program at the end of the interview process.

APPLYING FOR A HARDSHIP PROGRAM

Creditors do not advertise their hardship programs, so just call your credit card issuer and ask about what program that they may offer. Some customer service representatives from various banks, such as Chase and Discover Card, are empowered to offer credit card assistance right over the phone. In the interview process that will occur, you will have to tell the company about your sources of income, your expenses, and other financial obligations. You need to be prepared and to make sure that you have all your information ready before you call. You can expect that the creditors will want to know about how you're going to pay off your bills and eliminate your debt, and they will also want to know what caused your hardship. For step-by-step directions and tips on applying for and negotiating a hardship program with your creditor, see Chapter 6.

CONSUMER CREDIT COUNSELING

Consumer credit counseling (CCC), also known as a debt management plan (DMP), defined simply, is when debt is reduced through the managing of consumer assets and direct negotiation with creditors, to lower interest rates and payments on your unsecured bills. Debt management is offered by a licensed consumer credit counseling agency or a certified debt management company.

CCC agencies use DMPs, which are guidelines set by the creditors. DMPs offer consumers the ability to become debt-free in 3 to 6 years through creditors agreeing to lower consumers' interest rates and requiring the same payment amount from the first payment until completion. By negotiating lower interest rates with the consumer's existing creditors, much more of the consumer's payment can be applied to the principal, instead of the majority of the payment being applied to interest. The client's accounts will be closed by the creditors, and it is not recommended that clients pursue any additional credit or financing for at least 12 to 24 months.

A DMP entails a series of steps, which the CCC agency works on with the help of the consumer. The first step involves compiling a list of all your creditors and the amounts owed to each. Some creditors are not eligible to be included in a DMP. All accounts need to be open for a minimum of 6 to 9 months before they can have a proposal sent to the creditor to receive benefits. The following type of unsecured debt can be included in a DMP:

➢ Credit card debt

➢ Medical bills

➢ Payday loans

➢ Student loans

HISTORY OF CCC

The first credit counseling agencies were created in 1951 in the United States when credit grantors created The National Foundation for Credit Counseling (NFCC). According to W. Patrick Boisclair, Chairman of the NFCC's Board of Trustees, "the NFCC initially monitored legislative and regulatory activity for its retail credit members" and "also conducted public awareness campaigns on credit." Their stated objective was to promote financial literacy and help consumers avoid bankruptcy, but they did not serve as collection agencies for the creditors. The first local credit counseling franchises emerged in the 1960s, offering education and counseling directly to consumers.

In 1993, the Association of Independent Consumer Credit Counseling Agencies (AICCCA) was founded, citing a need for "industry-wide standards of excellence and ethical conduct." This formally organized the NFCC's competition. The AICCCA was formed from the group of counselors who favored telephone delivery of debt management programs. The NFCC was, in the beginning, strongly opposed to this telephone business model, primarily favoring face-to-face counseling as a more effective solution. Eventually, all organizations practiced both phone and face-to-face processes with some agencies using large inbound call centers driven by mass media advertising.

The credit counseling industry's third major trade organization is its largest: the American Association of Debt Management Organizations (AADMO).

However, all credit counseling agencies do not belong to a trade organization, nor are they required to do so. There are well over 1,000 active credit counseling organizations in the United States.

In 2005, the Bankruptcy Abuse Prevention and Consumer Protection Act of 2005 made credit counseling a requirement for consumer debtors filing for bankruptcy in the United States. In order to meet this requirement, during the 180-day period preceding the filing of bankruptcy, the debtor must complete a program with an approved nonprofit budget and credit counseling agency. Such a program may include, but is not limited to, one counseling session conducted by phone or over the Internet. In addition, a post-filing debtor education credit counseling session is required in order to complete the bankruptcy process and to have your debts discharged.

COMMON FEATURES OF CCC

After joining a CCC agency, the creditors will close the customer's accounts and restrict the accounts to future charges. The most common benefit of a DMP as advertised by most agencies is the consolidation of multiple monthly payments into one monthly payment, which is usually less than the sum of the individual payments previously paid by the consumer. This is because creditors will usually accept a lower monthly payment from a customer in a DMP than if the customer were paying the account on their own. Some DMPs advertise that payments can be cut by 50%, although a reduction of 10% to 20% is more common.

The second feature of a DMP is a reduction in interest rates charged by creditors. A customer with a defaulted credit card account will often be paying an interest rate approaching 30%. Upon joining a DMP, credit card banks sometimes lower the annual percentage rates charged to 5% to 10%, and a few eliminate interest altogether. This reduction in interest allows the CCC agencies to advertise that their customers will be debt-free in periods of 3 to 6 years, rather than the 20-plus years that it would take to pay off a large amount of debt with high interest rates.

A third benefit offered by CCC agencies is the process of bringing delinquent accounts current. This is often called "re-aging," or "curing," an account, and usually occurs after making a series of on-time payments through the DMP as a show of commitment to completing the program. For example, a client with an account with a monthly payment of $50 that has not been paid in 2 months might be considered by the creditor to be 60 days past due. After joining the DMP and making three consecutive monthly payments, the creditor could re-age the account to reflect a current status. Thereafter, the monthly payment due on the statements would be the monthly payment negotiated by the

DMP, and the account report as current to the credit bureaus. This process does not eliminate the prior delinquencies from the credit bureau reports; it merely gives a fresh start and an opportunity for the consumer to begin building a positive credit history. Like all negative credit information, the passage of time will lessen the impact of the negative marks when credit scores are calculated.

CRITICISM OF CCC

In the late 1980s and early 1990s, the number of credit and debt counseling agencies in America increased significantly. An antitrust lawsuit was filed against the NFCC, arguing that the presence of creditors on the NFCC's Board of Directors constituted monopolistic practices. As a result of this litigation, creditors agreed to fund non-NFCC member agencies as well.

These sharp increases of credit counseling activity also created other, more serious issues in the industry. By the early 1990s, abuses by certain credit counseling organizations were so significant, it led to criticism of the entire industry.

A credit counseling agency typically receives most of its compensation from the creditors to whom the debt payments are distributed. This funding relationship has led many to believe that credit counseling agencies are merely a soft collections wing of the creditors. This fee income, known as "Fair Share," consists of contributions from the creditors that originally earned the agency 15% of the amount recovered. However, in recent years, Fair Share contributions have dwindled steadily, with contributions of 4% to 10% being the most common.

Still, the NFCC considers bankcard companies to be one of their primary "constituents," and the NFCC website promotes the fact that they collect $5 billion for creditors each year. It also promotes their efforts to steer consumers away from bankruptcy.

The Federal Trade Commission has filed lawsuits against several CCC agencies and continues to urge caution in choosing one. The FTC has received more than 8,000 complaints from consumers about credit counselors—many concerning high or hidden fees and the inability to opt out of so-called voluntary contributions. The Better Business Bureau also reports high complaint levels about CCC agencies.

The IRS also has weighed in on the subject of credit counseling, and has denied nonprofit 501(c)(3) tax-exempt status to around 30 of the nation's 1000 CCC agencies. Those 30 credit counseling agencies account for more than half of the industry's revenue. Audits of nonprofit credit counseling agencies by the IRS are ongoing.

Other organizations have voiced criticisms of the credit counseling industry, often citing the "Fair Share" funding model as evidence that credit counselors serve the interests of the creditors over the interests of consumers, and that credit counselors are not forthcoming in speaking out about the actions of creditors for fear of losing what little funding remains. Credit counselors respond that their job is not to take sides but to negotiate with all parties equally to help successfully resolve debts. They further argue that the steady decline in "Fair Share" funding belies the notion that creditors are in control of the credit counseling industry.

Another common criticism of credit counseling is the assertion that participating in a DMP will ruin a consumer's credit. Fair Isaac Corporation, the company that pioneered the use of credit scores, states that participation in a DMP has no effect on a consumer's FICO credit score. However, the participation in such a plan may appear on consumer credit reports, and the consumer may have more difficulty obtaining a car or home loan and be denied any further unsecured credit, such as a credit card. That's because lenders often use multiple risk factors to determine creditworthiness. The major factor holding consumers back is the amount of debt they have relative to their income (the debt-to-income ratio), not enrollment in a credit counseling plan. While credit card banks offering relatively low-credit-line cards may use a credit score alone to approve a new account, a mortgage or car lender typically will scrutinize the entire credit report extensively and verify employment and income information. Some lenders view a prospective customer's participation in a DMP as indicative of the customer being unfit to manage their finances.

Additionally, mortgage loans backed by federal programs such as HUD or FHA have additional government underwriting guidelines in addition to the lender's own policies. HUD/FHA states their position on credit counseling is neutral and that a factor they will consider is whether the client has been adhering to the payment plan initially established through the CCC agency. The FHA recommends credit counseling programs to those who fear being denied a mortgage loan due to credit approval.

CCC agencies have also been criticized for understating their clients' future responsibilities during the initial enrollment process. Agencies have been accused of telling clients to stop paying creditors directly and to then keep the first payment made by the client into the DMP to cover fees. The result: Accounts being charged off during the period that the client transitions into the DMP. Many clients come to the DMP with current accounts; they are simply seeking lower interest rates rather than needing help bringing their accounts current. Since a DMP is designed for consumers who are having trouble meeting obligations, most consumers joining a DMP already has past-due accounts. For consumers who do not have past-due accounts, they should be aware that creditors will carry their accounts past due in exhange for a concession on the amount of interest charged. In this way, a client's credit can be damaged as the accounts unintentionally fall past due.

Given this criticism, the CCC industry is likely to be changed forever in the immediate future as it is scrutinized by both the consumer and government regulators over how they will be paid for the services they perform. In meantime, there will be no shortage of debt-burdened consumers who will now be facing a burgeoning, and more traditional, collection industry.

CAUTIONS REGARDING CCC

Consumers need to do their homework about credit counseling services before entering into an agreement. Consumers should shop around and compare services of CCC agencies and take note of the different fee structures of for-profit and not-for-profit agencies, as well as what services are offered for those fees. Consumers considering entering into a DMP should also be aware that their credit rating will may be impacted negatively and that their credit report may show that they used credit counseling. Prospective lenders, employers, and landlords may view information in an individual's credit report, if the application forms that the consumer signs grant them permission to do so.

BENEFITS OF CCC

The many benefits of CCC include:

> Lower monthly debt payments.

> Lower interest rates.

> Late charges and over-limit fees are waived.

> Stops harassing collection calls.

> You make only a single monthly payment to pay your bills.

> Eliminate your debt in 3 to 6 years.

> Minimal negative impact on your credit score.

CHOOSING A CCC AGENCY

Choosing a CCC agency is not something that should be taken lightly. What do you look for when choosing a CCC agency? Although they're dozens of factors to consider, these seven tips can make the process less stressful and may get you much closer to financial comfort faster and easier than you ever thought possible.

Get a Referral. Ask someone who has been in a similar situation. Take time to ask questions and to determine if they had a good or a bad experience with a particular firm. Getting information directly from another consumer who has used credit counseling in the past is an excellent way to learn before you agree to pay for services. In addition, a reputable company should be willing to provide examples of good results, without revealing another person's private information.

National Accreditation. While no specific national or state accreditation will guarantee success, there are organizations in the U.S. with the sole purpose of promoting high standards and ethical practices in the consumer credit industry. The American Association of Debt Management Organizations is one of the most prominent in this industry. Members of this organization specialize in credit counseling, debt management plans, budget/finance industry education, and much more.

Better Business Bureau Membership. Contact the Better Business Bureau in your city or region and ask for information about the credit counselor or debt management firm you are considering. You may also want to talk to someone in the State's Attorney or Attorney General's office to see if the company has been the subject of any regulatory action. Finally, check with the Better Business Bureau online to see the company's rating and review any complaints against it.

For-profit vs. Nonprofit Experience. Many consumers have a misunderstanding about not-for-profit debt management companies vs. for-profit companies. They both offer concessions for the consumer, whereas some states require nonprofit status before the company can do business in the state. Credit card companies fund most not-for-profit credit counseling companies with grants and fair-share deductions as a way for them to recover money from consumers who are currently not making their payments. The biggest difference? A not-for-profit organization doesn't pay taxes whereas a for-profit does. Study the company carefully to see if it uses the nonprofit status simply as a marketing tool. In addition, you should select a company that has been in business for a number of years.

Excessive Costs. In recent years, credit card companies and other lenders have reduced some of the funding for credit counseling. This has led counseling firms to increase their fees. Some of these increases are reasonable, but consumers should be careful not to get involved with a company that charges a large upfront payment just to establish an account. A baseline of $50 per month is a good guideline for an initial new debt management plan. In contrast, a credit counselor or debt manager should probably not charge a fee of more than $100 to establish your account and negotiate with your creditors. Some companies will waive their initial enrollment fees entirely if you can't afford them.

Real Education. Try to find a credit counselor or debt management professional who is sincere about giving you information that will help you deal with financial problems. You should not have to pay extra for CDs or videos that require you to learn on your own. If the person you are talking with does not or cannot provide satisfactory answers to your questions, find another company. Online access to necessary credit/debit forms and article information on the inner workings of credit and debt counseling should also be made available to you when possible.

A Written Plan. A reputable credit counseling firm or debt management company will take time to review your situation, help you with budgeting and money management, and put your individual plan in writing. This personalized plan should include details on how creditors will be paid, as well as realistic goals for returning you to full financial health. Some firms even offer a free debt comparison quote which is an excellent way to see how much money you can save, what your new interest rate may be, and how long it will take you to get debt-free on your debt consolidation program right out of the gate. Unrealistic promises should not be part of the plan. For example, a debt management or credit-counseling firm does not have the authority to change your credit report nor should it ever imply it has done so for clients in the past.

CCC agencies do not have any more influence in the negotiating of your interest rate than you do. Most consumers are unaware that they have the legal right to directly contact the creditor to negotiate their interest rates and payment plan. So, before taking these above few steps toward resolving credit or debt troubles, look closely at Chapter 6 to determine if you want to save hundreds of dollars by negotiating directly with your creditors. If so, you may be able to rebuild your credit and handle your debt situation privately without the assistance of a CCC agency. If this is not possible, it may be time to call a professional to help.

DEBT SETTLEMENT

Debt settlement, also known as debt arbitration or debt negotiation, is when the debtor and creditor agree on a reduced balance that will be regarded as payment in full.

If you are delinquent or having trouble paying your creditors, and the payments of a debt management plan do not fit into your monthly budget, you should consider debt settlement. When successful, you can eliminate anywhere from 40% to 55% of the outstanding balance. However, as long as debtors (consumers) continue to make minimum monthly payments, creditors will not negotiate to reduce the principal balance. Therefore, if you are considering debt settlement you will have to voluntarily decide to stop paying your creditors. Be advised, when payments stop, balances continue to grow because of late fees and ongoing interest.

Consumers can arrange their own settlements by using advice found in Chapter 7, hire a lawyer to act for them, or use debt settlement companies. In a *New York Times* article, Cyndi Geerdes, an associate professor at the University of Illinois Law School, states "Done correctly, [debt settlement] can absolutely help people." However, some settlement companies may charge a large fee up front, or take a monthly fee from customer bank accounts for their service—possibly reducing the incentive to settle with creditors quickly.

DEBT SETTLEMENT HISTORY

Lenders have been negotiating and settling debts for a number of years. However, the business of debt settlement became prominent in America during the late 1980s and early 1990s when bank deregulation was enacted, which loosened consumer lending practices, followed by an economic recession that placed consumers in financial hardships.

With charge-offs (debts written off by banks) increasing, banks established debt settlement departments staffed with personnel who were authorized to negotiate with defaulted cardholders to reduce the outstanding balances in hopes of recovering funds that would otherwise be lost if the cardholder filed for Chapter 7 Bankruptcy. Typical settlements range between 25% and 65% of the outstanding balance.

Alongside the unprecedented spike in personal debt loads, there has been another rather significant change—the 2005 passage of legislation that dramatically worsened the chances for average Americans to claim Chapter 7 bankruptcy protection. As things stand, should anyone filing for bankruptcy fail to meet the Internal Revenue Service regulated "means test," they would instead have to file a Chapter 13 debt restructuring plan. Essentially, Chapter 13 bankruptcies simply tell borrowers that they must pay back some or all of their debts to all unsecured lenders. Repayments under Chapter 13 can range from 1% to 100% of the amounts owed to unsecured creditors, based on the ability of the debtor to pay. Repayment periods are 3 years (for those who earn below the median income) or 5 years (for those above), under court-mandated budgets that follow IRS guidelines, and the penalties for failure are more severe.

HOW DEBT SETTLEMENT WORKS

Essentially, debt settlement is the process of negotiating with creditors to reduce overall debts in exchange for a lump sum payment. A successful settlement occurs when the creditor agrees to forgive a percentage of the total account balance. Only unsecured debts not secured by real assets like homes or automobiles can be settled. Unsecured debts include:

- ➢ Credit cards
- ➢ Medical bills
- ➢ Unsecured loans
- ➢ Unsecured personal loans
- ➢ Unsecured personal lines of credit
- ➢ Collections, and autos in repossession

Debt that cannot be included:

- ➢ Home loans/mortgages
- ➢ Auto loans and student loans
- ➢ Government loans
- ➢ Lawsuits, IRS debt/taxes
- ➢ Secured debts

For the debtor, this makes obvious sense; they avoid the stigma and intrusive court-mandated controls of bankruptcy while still lowering, sometimes by more than 50%, their debt balances. Whereas, for the creditor, they regain trust that the borrower intends to pay back what he/she can of the loans and not file bankruptcy (in which case, the creditor risks losing all monies owed).

Negotiating with a collection agency or debt buyer is somewhat similar to negotiating with a creditor directly. However, many collection agencies and debt buyers will agree to take less of the amount owed than the original creditor. Collection agencies work on a contingency fee basis; they do not want to spend too much time collecting on an account and in many cases would rather settle the account quickly and move onto the next account. Oftentimes, the creditor will sell the accounts to a debt buyer—accounts may be sold for an average of $0.15 on the dollar, in which case debt can be negotiated at a very good price.

When negotiating with a collection agency or debt buyer, as a part of the settlement, the consumer should request that collection be removed from the credit report, which generally won't happen with the original creditor. But even if the collection account from the consumer credit report has been successfully removed as a condition of settlement during negotiations, the negative marks from the original credit card company will still remain, according to Maxine Sweet, a spokeswoman for credit reporting agency Experian.

PROFESSIONAL DEBT SETTLEMENT

In order to work with a debt settlement professional, a consumer needs lump sum cash (best scenario), or needs to build up enough funds over a pre-determined period of time. For consumers who don't have the cash to make a lump sum settlement offer, debt settlement companies set up a third-party "trust" account where funds accumulate for the settlement process. A legitimate company will use an FDIC-insured trust account, generally through Global Client Solutions or Note World. Once enough funds are built up, the negotiation process can begin with each creditor individually.

POSITIVE SIDE OF USING A DEBT SETTLEMENT PROFESSIONAL

In many cases, consumers simply do not have the discipline to set aside the funds that are necessary to settle their accounts and need the structure that a debt settlement company offers. In other instances, a debt settlement company can offer advice to you on how to handle collection calls or ease your mind during the stressful times. Settlement companies generally package their settlements into a larger bulk settlement with the creditor for 35% to 50% of the existing balances. The debt settlement companies typically have built up a relationship with the creditors and can come to a settlement agreement quicker and at a more favorable rate than a consumer acting on their own. With the current economic crises, more and more creditors are willing to settle existing credit card debts rather than add to their already large written-off bad debt.

NEGATIVE SIDE OF USING A DEBT SETTLEMENT PROFESSIONAL

Debt settlement companies generally charge a fee of 10% to 18% of the total debt being placed in a debt settlement program. Credit card accounts typically go into collection after they are charged off, which occurs 180 days after the last payment on the account. During this time, the debt settlement companies may not handle calls from the credit card companies nor the collection agencies, as they do not have sufficient funds to negotiate with. Because of this, the drop-out rate of debt settlement programs is around 30% (the average length of the program is 36 months). During that time, consumers start becoming overwhelmed with collection calls. They may receive a settlement offer and realize they can settle the debt themselves, or creditors may file a lawsuit.

A traditional debt settlement company cannot represent their clients in court because they are not attorneys. Attorneys practicing debt settlement typically have a clause in their service agreement that states they "do not represent their clients in court regarding creditor lawsuits. However, they will attempt to settle the lawsuit outside of court." That's means if the lawsuit is not settled, consumers are left to defend themselves or hire another attorney to represent them. Other consumers simply cannot afford the debt settlement program any longer and may have to file for bankruptcy.

Entering into a debt settlement program does not mean that creditors seeking to recover debts and interest will not sue to recover their losses. But this risk can be minimized and possibly avoided by using attorneys or companies with good standings and practices that protect consumers from these procedures.

CHOOSING A DEBT SETTLEMENT PROFESSIONAL

If you are among the many who are considering hiring a professional to assist with debt settlement, this decision shouldn't be taken lightly—especially given the financial frauds going on during this economic downturn.

When deciding on a debt settlement provider, you do not need to choose an attorney; a debt settlement company will be sufficient or you can do it on your own (see Chapter 7 for step-by-step instructions).

That said, we recommend that consumers retain the services of an attorney with experience in the financial industry, specifically credit, collections, debt adjusting, and debt negotiations. By doing so you may incur a slightly higher fee than hiring a non-attorney debt settlement company, also known as a traditional debt settlement company. However, attorneys generally have a stronger presence when it comes to the art of negotiations and will likely offset those slightly higher fees with additional savings. Ultimately, an attorney could save you thousands of dollars because they are far less likely to take your money and not provide you with a service. The following are just a few reasons we strongly recommend an attorney over a traditional debt settlement company:

➢ Attorneys are held to a higher standard through the Attorney Ethics Committee and American Bar Association and could be suspended and/or disbarred for unethical practice of law or misappropriation of client funds.

➢ Attorneys understand and can interpret the laws governing debt collections such as the Fair Debt Collection Practices Act (FDCPA), the Fair Credit Reporting Act (FCRA), and Federal Trade Commission (FTC).

➢ A stronger presence in negotiation when dealing with collection agencies or debt collection attorneys that generally lead to greater savings.

➢ At the time of writing this book, 26 states have laws preventing traditional debt settlement companies from participating in debt settlement: Colorado, District of Colombia, Hawaii, Iowa, Idaho, Kansas, Kentucky, Maine, Minnesota, Mississippi, Nevada, New Jersey, North Carolina, Ohio, Oregon, Pennsylvania, Wisconsin, Tennessee, Utah, Virginia, Vermont, Washington, and West Virginia.

   o Also, there is pending legislation, which, if passed into law, will prohibit traditional debt settlement companies (non-attorney) state-wide from participating in debt settlement. (See Chapter 4 for more details.)

TIPS IN HIRING A DEBT SETTLEMENT PROFESSIONAL

Associations. The company you are considering should be a member of the International Association of Debt Arbitrators or the United States Organization for Bankruptcy Alternatives (U.S.O.B.A). While no specific national or state accreditation will guarantee success, these are organizations in the U.S. with the sole purpose of promoting high standards and ethical practices in the consumer debt relief industry. They do provide credibility for the traditional debt settlement company. We recommend using an attorney who is associated with these organizations.

Excessive Costs. Consumers should *not* get involved with traditional companies that charge a baseline maintenance fee. Please note: If retaining an attorney, expect to pay a fee in the range of $49.95 to $69 per month.

Enrollment/Upfront Fees. Consumers should *not* get involved with traditional companies that charge upfront enrollment fees. Please note: If retaining an attorney, expect to pay a small retainer fee (in the range of $199 to $299).

Where Your money Is Being Held. Consumers should *not* get involved with companies that don't open a Special Purpose Accounts (SPA) with Global Client Solutions. These accounts are opened in the consumer's name and the consumer receives a monthly statement either online and/or by mail. These FDIC-insured accounts provide an extra layer of protection for the consumer. Please note: There is an approximate maintenance fee of $9.85 per month to maintain your SPA trust account.

Fees for Service. Service fees should *not* be paid upfront; they should be paid over a period of 12 to 18 months depending on the term of your program. Clients should have enough money in their SPA to settle at least one debt in the first 6 to 12 months. *Consumers should review the deposit schedule and all fees associated with any debt settlement program before signing any agreement.*

Written Plan. Consumers should *not* get involved with companies that won't take the time to review their situation, help them with budgeting and money management, and put their individual plan in writing. Unrealistic promises should not be part of the plan. For example, a counselor should always advise you of the negative impact on your credit score. Also, no company has the authority to change your credit report nor should it ever imply it has done so in the past. Additionally, they should never promise a specific amount of possible savings; everything is an estimate as there is no guarantee with debt settlement, there is only a "best efforts" basis.

Cancelation/Return Policy. There should be a money-back guarantee in the agreement. This usually gives the consumer 30 days to cancel.

Recording Compliance Call. Consumers should *not* get involved with companies that don't conduct a recorded compliance call to verify you have a clear understanding of the debt settlement program that you have entered into. This call insures that the debt counselor covered all the key components of the debt settlement program you have entered into and did not use deceptive measures to entice you into signing the agreement.

Hiring a debt settlement company won't stop the collection calls. Nor will it stop interest and financing charges from continuing to build up, and lenders may even decide to sue in the meantime. Some credit card companies often refuse to negotiate with debt settlement companies. Debt settlement does have a negative impact on the consumer's credit score.

Attorneys and debt settlement companies do not have any more influence in the negotiating debt than the consumer. Most consumers are unaware that they have the legal right to directly contact the creditor to negotiate their debt. So, before hiring a professional for resolving credit or debt difficulties, look closely at Chapter 7 to determine if you want to save hundreds or maybe thousands of dollars by negotiating directly with your creditors.

SNAPSHOT OF DO-IT-YOURSELF DEBT SETTLEMENT

As we said, it is possible for a consumer to imitate the methods of professional debt settlement companies. Many people report success in negotiating a debt settlement for themselves. Initiation of negotiations can begin by preparing your case, which are legitimate reasons for being delinquent. Among the valid reasons are:

➢ Job loss

➢ Loss of income

➢ Divorce

➢ Medical emergency

➢ Natural Disasters

Call the customer service department of the credit card company and ask to speak with a supervisor or the hardship/settlement department. Explain your financial crises and make a settlement offer. Start negotiations at 30% with an end goal of 50%. Usually a payment plan is not an option, but credit card companies may be willing to do a settlement over 3 to 6 months; the credit card company will always demand that the consumer make a lump sum payment of the settlement amount. After agreeing on a settlement price, ask the creditor to report to all three major credit bureaus that the account has been paid in full.

Use the payment as a negotiating tool; oftentimes, the creditor will agree to a positive listing for payment in hand. Before making your payment make sure the creditor provides you with all the settlement details in writing. Once you have it in writing, issue payment to the creditor.

THE POSITIVE SIDE OF DO-IT-YOURSELF DEBT SETTLEMENT

By negotiating debts on their own, consumers are able to save themselves a great deal in fees that would otherwise be paid to a debt settlement company or an attorney. This option also gives the debtor more control over the process which may, or may not, be a motivational factor to continue successfully completing the process.

THE NEGATIVE SIDE OF DO-IT-YOURSELF DEBT SETTLEMENT

While the do-it-yourself option offers the consumer more control and reduced fees, there are negatives generally associated with this option. Every creditor has different processes and procedures in how they determine settlement offers and terms given. Not knowing those can leave a consumer in the dark, facing less advantageous settlement rates on their own, as opposed to debt settlement companies that may have built relationships with creditors from previous settlements and can often package bulk settlements.

Creditors may become very intimidating and aggressive and accounts may escalate to legal status. The unfamiliarity of the settlement process can be intimidating and mistakes can be made. You will need to beware of fine print and carefully review any correspondence, proposed settlement, or agreements with a creditor. Settling one's debt can be an emotionally draining and difficult process. If you are considering debt settlement, please refer to Chapter 7, which gives an in-depth look and step-by-step instructions to overcome the negative pitfalls associated with do-it-yourself debt settlement.

CREDITOR INCENTIVES

The creditor's primary incentive is to recover funds that would otherwise be lost if the debtor filed for bankruptcy. The other key incentive is that the creditor can often recover more funds than through other collection methods.

Collection agencies and collection attorneys charge a commission upwards of 40% on recovered funds. Debt buyers purchase portfolios of delinquent debts from creditors who give up on internal collection efforts and these debt buyers pay between 1 and 20 cents on the dollar, depending on the age of the debt, with the oldest debts being the cheapest. Collection calls and lawsuits sometimes push debtors into bankruptcy, in which case the creditor often recovers no funds.

COMMON OBJECTIONS OF DEBT SETTLEMENT

Damages Credit. Credit reports will show evidence of debt settlements and the associated FICO scores will be lowered temporarily as a result. However, if a "paid in full" letter is obtained from the creditor, the debtor's credit report should show no sign of a debt settlement. Additionally, as debtors settle their accounts the score starts to go back up again. Some debt settlement companies offer credit repair in their programs in order to erase some of the negative remarks on credit reports. Please be advised, if the negative remarks in the report are accurate, most likely they will not be removed except through time.

Potential for Lawsuits. Though few creditors wish to push borrowers toward bankruptcy (and the potential of governmental protection against all debts), there's always the possibility of a lawsuit whenever debts remain unpaid. In the debt settlement process the debtor's accounts remain in default. While the debts are still in default the creditor or its assignee can still file a lawsuit against a consumer. Most creditors and debt collectors want a lump sum payment to settle for less than the full debt. Although a consumer may make monthly payments to the debt settlement company, the amount may be too small to successfully negotiate a settlement until after the consumer has made several months' worth of payments (usually 6 to 12 payments).

Eligibility of Debts. The specific debts of the borrowers themselves affect the success of negotiations. Tax liens and domestic judgments remain unaffected by attempts at settlement. Student loans, even those not federally subsidized, have been granted special powers by recent legislation to attach bank accounts without possibility of Chapter 7 bankruptcy protection. Also, some individual creditors, including Discover Card, for example, tend to have an aggressive resistance against negotiations.

Tax Consequences. Another common objection to debt settlement is that debtors whose debts are partially canceled outside the bankruptcy system will need to report the canceled portion of the debt as taxable income (IRS Publication Form 982). The Internal revenue Service (IRS) considers $600 or more of forgiven debt as taxable income. The forgiving creditor must provide the taxpayer with a 1099-C tax form. This form will list the amount of forgiven debt and interest in Box 2. Taxpayers with portions of personal loans forgiven may not subtract the interest reported in Box 3 from the amount of reportable income on this form.

However, the IRS does not require taxpayers to report forgiven debt if the tax payer was insolvent at the time the creditor forgave the debt. Being insolvent means that the amount of a debtor's debts are greater than his/her assets (how much money and property the debtor owns). However, the IRS adds that "you cannot exclude any amount of canceled debt that is more than the amount by which you are insolvent."

For example, if a taxpayer is $10,000 in debt and owns $3,000 in assets, he/she cannot exclude more than $7,000 of forgiven debt from his/her income tax. Any forgiven debt over $7,000 that year must be reported as taxable income.

DEBT SETTLEMENT TRADE ASSOCIATIONS

Due to the rise of debt settlement as a debt relief alternative to bankruptcy, groups working in the industry have established trade associations to help secure industry standards that will protect consumers against unethical business practices. These trade associations were also established to lobby state governments because many state legislatures have been passing laws that restrict out-of-state companies from providing debt negotiation services to in-state residents. The primary trade association is the United States Organization for Bankruptcy Alternatives (USOBA). This organization publishes on their websites information about debt settlement and the debt settlement industry. Individual debt settlement consultants receive certification training (accreditation) from the International Association of Professional Debt Arbitrators (IAPDA).

BANKRUPTCY

Bankruptcy has the most detrimental impact on your credit score and remains on your credit for 7 to 10 years. Bankruptcy should be an absolute last resort.

THE NEW BANKRUPTCY LAW

Under the old rules, people who filed under Chapter 13 had to devote all of their disposable income, what they had left after paying their actual living expenses, to their repayment plan. The new law adds a wrinkle to this equation: Although Chapter 13 filers still have to hand over all of their disposable income, they have to calculate their disposable income using allowed expense amounts dictated by the IRS, not their actual expenses, if their income is higher than the median in their state (see "Restricted Eligibility for Chapter 7," below). These expenses are often lower than actual costs.

What's worse, these allowed expense amounts must be subtracted not from the filer's actual earnings each month, but from the filer's average income during the 6 months before filing. This means that debtors may be required to pay a much larger amount of "disposable income" into their plan than they actually have to spare every month, which, in turn, means that many more Chapter 13 plans will fail.

PROPERTY MUST BE VALUED AT REPLACEMENT COST

Under the old law, Chapter 7 filers could value their property at what they could sell it for in a "fire sale" or auction. This meant that used furniture, hobby items, cars, heirlooms, and other property a debtor might want to keep were typically assumed to have little value and, therefore, that it often fell well within the "exempt property" categories offered by most states. (Exempt property is property that cannot be taken by creditors or the trustee; you are entitled to keep it.)

Under the new law, you must value your property at what it would cost to replace it from a retail vendor, taking into account the property's age and condition. This requirement is sure to jack up the value of property, which means more debtors stand to have their property taken and sold by the trustee.

RESTRICTED ELIGIBILITY FOR CHAPTER 7

Under the old rules, most filers could choose the type of bankruptcy that seemed best for them and most chose Chapter 7 over Chapter 13. The new law will prohibit some filers with higher incomes from using Chapter 7.

HOW HIGH IS YOUR INCOME?

Under the new rules, the first step in figuring out whether you can file for Chapter 7 is to measure your "current monthly income" against the median income for a family of your size in your state. Your "current monthly income" is not your income at the time you file, however: it is your average income over the last 6 months before you file. For many people, particularly those who are filing for bankruptcy because they recently lost a job, their "current monthly income" according to these rules will be much more than they take in each month by the time they file for bankruptcy.

Once you've calculated your income, compare it to the median income for your state. You can find median income tables, by state and family size, at the United States Trustee website:

➤ http://www.justice.gov/ust/

➤ http://www.justice.gov/ust/eo/bapcpa/meanstesting.htm)

If your income is less than or equal to the median, you can file for Chapter 7. If it is more than the median, however, you must pass "the means test," another requirement of the new law, in order to file for Chapter 7.

THE MEANS TEST

The purpose of the means test is to figure out whether you have enough disposable income, after subtracting certain allowed expenses and required debt payments, to make payments on a Chapter 13 plan.

To find out whether you pass the means test, you start with your "current monthly income," calculated as described above. From that amount, you subtract both of the following:

➤ Certain allowed expenses, in amounts set by the IRS. Generally, you cannot subtract what you actually spend for things like transportation, food, clothing, and so on; instead, you have to use the limits the IRS imposes, which may be lower than the cost of living in your area.

➤ Monthly payments, which you will have to make on secured and priority debts. Secured debts are those for which the creditor is entitled to seize property if you don't pay (such as a mortgage or car loan); priority debts are obligations that the law deems to be so important that they are entitled to jump to the head of the repayment line. Typical priority debts include child support, alimony, tax debts, and wages owed to employees.

If your total monthly disposable income after subtracting these amounts is less than $100, you pass the means test, and will be allowed to file for Chapter 7. If your total remaining monthly disposable income is more than $166.66, you have flunked the means test, and will be prohibited from using Chapter 7. So what about those in the middle? If your remaining monthly disposable

DIG YOURSELF OUT OF DEBT

income is between $100 and $166.66, you must figure out whether what you have left over is enough to pay more than 25% of your unsecured, non-priority debts (such as credit card bills, student loans, medical bills, and so on) over a five-year period. If so, you flunk the means test, and Chapter 7 won't be available to you. If not, you pass the means test, and Chapter 7 remains an option.

REQUIREMENTS EASED FOR HURRICANE VICTIMS

Following Hurricanes Katrina and Rita, the United States Trustee's office announced special enforcement guidelines for debtors affected by natural disasters. These guidelines are an effort to lessen the impact of the new law on filers who may be displaced from their homes and personal papers.

Among other things, these guidelines make the following changes for victims of natural disasters who file for bankruptcy:

➢ Credit counseling will not be required.

➢ Debtors who cannot provide required documents due to a natural disaster will not face enforcement actions.

➢ Trustees are to consider the income loss, increased expenses, and other effects of a natural disaster as "special circumstances" that may allow a debtor who doesn't otherwise pass the means test to qualify for Chapter 7.

➢ Trustees will provide alternate means for debtors to attend creditors' meetings, if necessary.

For more on these rules, go to the website of the United States Trustee at www.usdoj.gov/ust and click "Enforcement Guidelines for Debtors Affected by Natural Disasters."

LAWYERS MAY BE HARDER TO FIND AND MORE EXPENSIVE

As you can see, the new law adds some complicated requirements to the field of bankruptcy. This is going to make it more expensive and time consuming for lawyers to represent clients in bankruptcy cases, which means attorney fees have gone up.

The new law also imposes some additional requirements on lawyers, chief among them that the lawyer must personally vouch for the accuracy of all of the information their clients provide them. This means attorneys will have to spend even more time on bankruptcy cases, and charge their clients accordingly. Some experts predict that this combination of new requirements may drive some bankruptcy lawyers out of the field altogether.

STATE EXEMPTIONS AREN'T AVAILABLE TO RECENT STATE RESIDENTS

Under the old bankruptcy law, the personal property debtors were allowed to keep in Chapter 7 bankruptcy was determined by the laws of the state where they lived (as long as they lived there for at least 3 months). Under the new law, you must live in a state for at least 2 years before filing in order to use that state's exemption laws. Otherwise, you must use the exemptions available in the state where you used to live. Similar rules apply to homestead exemptions, which determine how much equity in a home you can keep when filing for Chapter 7 bankruptcy. However, to use your new state's homestead exemption, you must live there for at least 40 months.

Because exemption amounts vary widely from state to state, these new residency requirements could make a big difference in the amount of property you get to keep. For example, if you recently moved from California to Nevada and you have a fairly valuable car, you might want to wait to file for Chapter 7—once you've been in Nevada for 2 years, you can claim its $15,000 exemption for motor vehicles. If you have to use California's exemptions, you can keep only $2,300 worth of equity.

CHAPTER 4

THE CONTROVERSY, CRITICISM, AND SCAMS OF DEBT SETTLEMENT PROFESSIONALS

PROFESSIONAL DEBT SETTLEMENT

In order to work with a debt settlement professional, a consumer needs lump sum cash (best scenario), or needs to build up enough funds over a pre-determined period of time. For consumers who have no cash to make a lump sum settlement offer, debt settlement companies set up a third-party "trust" account where funds accumulate for the settlement process. A legitimate company will use an FDIC-insured trust account, generally through Global Client Solutions or Note World. Once enough funds are built up, the negotiation process can begin with each creditor individually.

POSITIVE SIDE OF USING A DEBT SETTLEMENT PROFESSIONAL

In many cases consumers simply do not have the discipline to set aside the funds that are necessary to settle their accounts and need the structure that a debt settlement company offers. In other instances a debt settlement company can offer advice to you on how to handle collection calls or maybe just ease your mind during the difficult and stressful times. Settlement companies generally package their settlements into a larger bulk settlement with the creditor for 35% to 50% of the existing balances. The reputable debt settlement companies typically have built up a relationship during their normal business practices with the creditors and can come to a settlement agreement quicker and at a more favorable rate than a consumer acting on their own. With the current economic crises, more and more creditors are willing to settle existing credit card debts rather than add to their already large written-off bad debt.

NEGATIVE SIDE OF USING A DEBT SETTLEMENT PROFESSIONAL

Debt settlement attorneys generally charge a fee of 15% of the total debt being placed in a debt settlement program, plus monthly service fees of at least $50 and an initial retainer. Credit card accounts typically go into collection after they are charged off, which occurs 180 days after the last payment on the account. During this time, the debt settlement companies may not handle calls from the credit card companies, nor the collection agencies, as they do not have sufficient funds to negotiate with. Because of this, the drop-out rate of debt settlement programs is around 30% since the average length of the program is 36 months. And during that time, consumers start becoming overwhelmed with collection calls. Consumers may receive a settlement offer and realize they can settle the debt themselves, or creditors may file a lawsuit.

A traditional debt settlement company cannot represent their clients in court because they are not attorneys. Attorneys practicing debt settlement typically have a clause in their service agreement that states "they do not represent their clients in court regarding creditor lawsuits. However, they will attempt to settle the lawsuit outside of court." Meaning if the lawsuit is not settled, consumers are left to defend themselves or hire another attorney to represent them. Other consumers simply cannot afford the debt settlement program any longer and may have to file for bankruptcy.

Entering into a debt settlement program does not mean that creditors seeking to recover debts and interest will not sue to recover their losses. This risk can be minimized and possibly avoided by using attorneys or companies with good standings and practices that protect consumers from these procedures.

CHOOSING A DEBT SETTLEMENT PROFESSIONAL

In choosing a debt settlement provider, you do not need an attorney to assist you; you can do it on your own.

If you are among the many who are considering hiring a professional to assist with debt settlement, don't take the decision lightly, given all the financial scams going on in this economic downturn.

We recommend that consumers retain the services of an attorney that will provide full representation and are experienced in consumer debt resolutions. By doing so you may incur a slightly higher fee than hiring an attorney that only offers partial representation. The difference between full and partial representation is as follows:

Services You Will Receive	Full Representation	Partial Representation
Negotiate with your creditors	Yes	Yes
Stop phone calls	Yes	No
Court representation if a creditor files a lawsuit	Yes	No
Representation if a creditor/collector violates state or federal collection laws	Yes	No
Offices in my state where I can meet with my attorney face-to-face	Yes	Maybe
File bankruptcy if necessary	Yes	Maybe

CONTROVERSY OF DEBT SETTLEMENT COMPANIES

The debt settlement industry has been under fire for a while now. Like many industries, there are great, good, and bad companies. However, the unscrupulous companies that take advantage of consumers while they are overwhelmed with debt and struggling to survive tend to stand out amongst all others. Unfortunately, there have always been predators lurking to take advantage of others when they at their weakest, and in a down economy, there are no shortage of predators or their prey. Many of these "bad" companies use fraudulent business practices and false advertising to lure consumers in. Once they get the consumer's attention, they do not fully disclose the necessary information to them. In most cases, the misrepresentation comes when discussing:

➤ Collection calls

➤ Impact on your credit score

➢ Interest and late fees

➢ The possibility that you may be sued

➢ How money is allocated

➢ When creditors will receive their money

➢ Promising or guaranteeing a specific settlement amount

Finding a reputable debt settlement company may be a daunting task: Consumers who are considering hiring a debt settlement company may find little help checking out those companies with the Better Business Bureau. "Under the BBB's new rating system, it is virtually impossible for a debt settlement company to be rated anything other than a 'D' or 'F'," warns The Association of Settlement Companies (TASC), the professional association for the debt settlement industry.

Debt settlement companies help consumers who cannot pay the full amount of their unsecured debts negotiate reduced payoffs or "settlements" with creditors. These companies are becoming a popular option for debt-strapped consumers who want to avoid bankruptcy but cannot pay back their full debts through credit counseling. With the economic downturn, the settlement industry is experiencing significant growth, while also attracting criticism from regulators concerned with high upfront fees and aggressive sales practices.

In a February letter, TASC sent to the National Council of Better Business Bureaus, the organization alleged that "there are critical flaws in the BBB's consumer grading system as it applies to settlement firms." The letter expressed concern that all settlement companies will be given poor ratings, regardless of the number of consumer complaints, how those complaints have been resolved, or the business practices of the settlement Firm under review.

TASC says the dispute stems from the fact that the BBB does not consider debt settlement a viable option for consumers who cannot afford to pay back their debts and want professional help to negotiate lower payments.

"We provide a valuable service for consumers and feel we have an obligation to regulate our members," said Chris Kesterson, TASC president and chief executive of Debt Settlement America in Dallas. "We think the Better Business Bureau is promoting a position that shuts out an important option for certain consumers struggling to manage their debt and get back on their financial feet."

In a written statement, the Council of Better Business Bureaus stated, "Debt negotiation/settlement businesses are downgraded in the BBB rating system based on BBB concerns with the debt negotiation/settlement industry. The FTC held a workshop on debt negotiation/settlement last fall, and similar concerns were expressed as to how the industry operates and the likelihood that debt negotiation/settlement benefits a significant number of consumers." The organization has indicated a willingness to review its rating system upon receipt of further documentation by TASC.

Until the matter is resolved, consumers should be aware that a debt settlement company's negative rating by the BBB may not reflect an individual agency's record of complaints. Consumers who are considering hiring a debt settlement firm must use their own due diligence and review contracts carefully before signing.
(**Source: 3/2009**, *http://www.fourpeaksfinancialservices.com/TASC/TASC_2.pdf*)

FTC ISSUES FINAL RULE TO PROTECT CONSUMER IN CREDIT CARD DEBT

Amendments to Telemarketing Sales Rule Prohibiting Debt Relief Companies from collecting Advance Fees went into effect in October 2010.

On October 27, 2010, for-profit companies that sell debt relief services over the telephone may no longer charge a fee before they settle or reduce a customer's credit card or other unsecured debt.

"At the FTC we strive every day to make sure America's middle class families get straight deals for their dollars," Chairman Jon Leibowitz said. "This rule will stop companies who offer consumers false promises of reducing credit card debts by half or more in exchange for large, up-front fees. Too many of these companies pick the last dollar out of consumers' pockets—and far from leaving them better off, push them deeper into debt, even bankruptcy."

The three additional Telemarketing Sales Rule provisions that went into effect on September 27, 2010, will:

- Require debt relief companies to make specific disclosures to consumers.

- Prohibit them from making misrepresentations.

- Extend the Telemarketing Sales Rule to cover calls consumers make to these firms in response to debt relief advertising.

The Final Rule covers telemarketers of for-profit debt relief services, including credit counseling, debt settlement, and debt negotiation services. The Final Rule does not cover nonprofit firms, but does cover companies that falsely claim nonprofit status. Over the past decade, the FTC and state enforcers have brought a combined 259 cases to stop deceptive and abusive practices by debt relief providers that have targeted consumers in financial distress.

Advance Fee Ban. The Final Rule contains specific requirements for debt relief providers related to charging an advance fee before providing any services. It specifies that fees for debt relief services may not be collected until:

- the debt relief service successfully renegotiates, settles, reduces, or otherwise changes the terms of at least one of the consumer's debts;

- there is a written settlement agreement, debt management plan, or other agreement between the consumer and the creditor, and the consumer has agreed to it; and

- the consumer has made at least one payment to the creditor as a result of the agreement negotiated by the debt relief provider.

To ensure that debt relief providers do not front-load their fees if a consumer has enrolled multiple debts in one debt relief program, the Final Rule specifies how debt relief providers can collect their fee for each settled debt. First, the provider's fee for a single debt must be in proportion to the total fee that would be charged if all of the debts had been settled. Alternatively, if the provider bases its fee on the percentage of what the consumer saves as result of using its services, the percentage charged must be the same for each of the consumer's debts.

Dedicated Account for Fees and Savings. Another new provision of the Final Rule will allow debt relief companies to require that consumers set aside their fees and savings for payment to creditors in a "dedicated account." However, providers may only require a dedicated account as long as five conditions are met:

- the dedicated account is maintained at an insured financial institution;

- the consumer owns the funds (including any interest accrued);

- the consumer can withdraw the funds at any time without penalty;

- the provider does not own or control or have any affiliation with the company administering the account; and

- the provider does not exchange any referral fees with the company administering the account.

Disclosures and Prohibited Misrepresentations. Under the Final Rule, providers will have to make several disclosures when telemarketing their services to consumers. Before the consumer signs up for any debt relief service, providers must disclose fundamental aspects of their services, including how long it will take for consumers to see results, how much it will cost, the negative consequences that could result from using debt relief services, and key information about dedicated accounts if they choose to require them.

The Final Rule also prohibits misrepresentations about any debt relief service, including success rates and whether the provider is a nonprofit entity. The FTC's Statement of Basis and Purpose, which accompanies the Final Rule, provides extensive guidance about the evidence providers must have to make advertising claims commonly used in selling debt relief services.

The Rulemaking Process. In August 2009, the FTC published in the Federal Register a notice of proposed rulemaking proposing amendments to the Telemarketing Sales Rule and requesting public comments; there were over 300 commenters, representing a wide variety of stakeholders. Commission also held a public forum on the proposed amendments on November 4, 2009. The FTC developed the Final Rule based on the public comments, the record of the public forum and the FTC's September, 2008 Workshop on the debt settlement industry, recent testimony before Congress, and law enforcement actions brought by the Commission and the states.

Information for Businesses. The FTC staff issued a compliance guide to help businesses comply with the new debt relief rules. The compliance guide describes the key changes to the Telemarketing Sales Rule affecting debt relief services, helps businesses determine if they are covered by the new rules, details information that covered entities must disclose to customers, and discusses how fees may now be collected.

The FTC vote approving publication of the Federal Register notice was 4-1, with Commissioner J. Thomas Rosch voting no.

The provisions of the Final Rule took effect on September 27, 2010, with the exception of the advance fee ban provision, which took effect on October 27, 2010. *(Source: FTC, http://www.ftc.gov/opa/2010/07/tsr.shtm)*

CHAPTER 5

DON'T BE INTIMIDATED BY COLLECTION AGENCIES: KNOW YOUR RIGHTS

KNOW YOUR RIGHTS

Creditors and collection agencies have rules governing their collection procedures both nationally through the Fair Debt Collection Practice Act (FDCPA) and locally through state laws. These laws govern several issues. They specify how and when and where a collector may contact you. The Federal Trade Commission (FTC) states that a collector may contact you by phone, fax, or mail. They can only contact you by phone between the hours of 8 a.m. and 9 p.m. Collectors may contact others associated with you such as friends, relatives, or your boss to leave a message, find out where you live, and obtain a phone number or find out where you work. They are prohibited from discussing the debt or amount of money owed. If they contact you at work and you advise them that you cannot receive such calls, they must honor your request not to contact you at work.

If you use credit cards, owe money on a personal loan, or are paying on a home mortgage, you are a "debtor." If you fall behind in repaying your creditors, or an error is made on your accounts, you may be contacted by a "debt collector."

You should know that in either situation, the FDCPA requires that debt collectors treat you fairly and prohibits certain methods of debt collection. Of course, the law does not erase any legitimate debt you owe. The following are questions commonly asked about your rights under the FDCPA.

What debts are covered?

Personal, family, and household debts are covered under the Act. This includes money owed for the purchase of an automobile, for medical care, or for charge accounts.

Who is a debt collector?

A debt collector is any person who regularly collects debts owed to others. This includes attorneys who collect debts on a regular basis.

How a debt collector may contact you?

A collector may contact you in person, by mail, telephone, telegram, or fax. However, a debt collector may not contact you at inconvenient times or places, such as before 8 a.m. or after 9 p.m., unless you agree. A debt collector also may not contact you at work if the collector knows that your employer disapproves of such contacts.

Can you stop a debt collector from contacting you?

You can stop a debt collector from contacting you by writing a letter to the collector telling them to stop. Once the collector receives your letter, they may not contact you again except to say there will be no further contact or to notify you that the debt collector or the creditor intends to take some specific action. Please note, however, that sending such a letter to a collector does not make the debt go away if you actually owe it. You could still be sued by the debt collector or your original creditor.

May a debt collector contact anyone else about your debt?

If you have an attorney, the debt collector must contact the attorney, rather than you. If you do not have an attorney, a collector may contact other people, but only to find out where you live, what your phone number is, and where you work. Collectors usually are prohibited from contacting such third parties more than once. In most cases, the collector may not tell anyone other than you and your attorney that you owe money.

What must the debt collector tell you about the debt?

Within five days after you are first contacted, the collector must send you a written notice telling you the amount of money you owe, the name of the creditor to whom you owe the money, and what action to take if you believe you do not owe the money.

May a debt collector continue to contact you if you believe you do not owe money?

A collector may not contact you if, within 30 days after you receive the written notice, you send the collection agency a letter stating you do not owe money. However, a collector can renew collection activities if you are sent proof of the debt, such as a copy of a bill for the amount owed.

Harassment. Debt collectors may not harass, oppress, or abuse you or any third parties they contact. For example, debt collectors may not:

- ✓ Use threats of violence or harm.

- ✓ Publish a list of consumers who refuse to pay their debts (except to a credit bureau.)

- ✓ Use obscene or profane language.

- ✓ Repeatedly use the telephone to annoy someone.

False Statements. Debt collectors may not use any false or misleading statements when collecting a debt. For example, debt collectors may not:

- ✓ Falsely imply that they are attorneys or government representatives.

- ✓ Falsely imply that you have committed a crime.

- ✓ Falsely represent that they operate or work for a credit bureau.

- ✓ Misrepresent the amount of your debt.

- ✓ Indicate that papers being sent to you are legal forms when they are not.

- ✓ Indicate that papers being sent to you are not legal forms when they are.

Debt collectors also may not state that:

- ✓ You will be arrested if you do not pay your debt.

- ✓ They will seize, garnish, attach, or sell your property or wages, unless the collection agency or creditor intends to do so, and it is legal to do so.

✓ Actions, such as a lawsuit, will be taken against you, when such action legally may not be taken, or when they do not intend to take such action.

Debt collectors may not:

✓ Give false credit information about you to anyone, including a credit bureau.

✓ Send you anything that looks like an official document from a court or government agency when it is not.

✓ Use a false name.

SNAPSHOT OF THE FAIR DEBT COLLECTION PRACTICES ACT

(As amended by Public Law 99-361 – July 9, 1986) Title 15 United Sates Code - Sections 1692 to 1692p

SECTION 805 – COMMUNICATION IN CONNECTION WITH DEBT COLLECTION

❖ Collectors may only call after 8:00 a.m. and no later than 9:00 p.m. (in your time zone).

❖ Collectors cannot contact you once you notify them that you are being represented by an attorney.

❖ Collectors may not call a consumer's place of employment, once the consumer advises that they are prohibited from receiving such calls.

❖ Collectors may not communicate account specifics with any person other than the consumer himself (unless authorized by the consumer or cosigner to do so). This includes all family members.

SECTION 806 – HARASSMENT OR ABUSE

❖ Collectors may not use threats of violence or other criminal means.

❖ Collectors may not use profanity.

❖ Collectors may not continuously call, annoy, abuse, or harass consumers.

SECTION 807 – FALSE OR MISLEADING REPRESENTATIONS

- ❖ Collectors may not use any false or deceptive or misleading representations.

- ❖ Collectors may not threaten to take any action that cannot legally be taken.

- ❖ Collectors may not give or threaten to give out false credit information.

- ❖ Collectors may not distribute any falsely written communication simulating any document authorized, issued, or approved by any court, official, or agency of the United States or any states.

- ❖ Collectors may not use any name other than the true name of the collector's business, company, or organization.

- ❖ Collectors may not falsely imply that they are employed by a consumer-reporting agency.

SECTION 808 – UNFAIR PRACTICES

- ❖ Collectors may not use unfair or unconscionable means to collect or attempt to collect any debt.

- ❖ Collectors cannot accept a check or other payment form from the consumer that is postdated by more than five days.

- ❖ Collectors may not solicit any postdated check for the purpose of threatening or instituting criminal prosecution.

- ❖ Collectors may not deposit or threaten to deposit any postdated check before the date on the check.

- ❖ Collectors may not cause charges to be made to the consumer for the price of communication.

- ❖ Collectors may not take or threaten to take non-judicial action to effect dispossession or disablement of property.

- ❖ Collectors may not communicate with a consumer by postcard.

- ❖ Collectors may not use any language or symbol other than the collector's address and name on any mail sent to the consumer.

SECTION 809 – VALIDATION OF DEBTS

❖ Collectors must notify the consumer in writing within five (5) days, validating their debt.

SECTION 810 – MULTIPLE DEBTS

❖ If a consumer owes multiple debts to one creditor and makes a payment to the collector for one specific debt, the collector may not apply such payment to any disputed debt and MUST apply the payment as the consumer directs.

(Source: http://www.ftc.gov/os/statutes/fdcpa/fdcpact.shtm)

DIFFERENT DEBT COLLECTORS

Collectors must identify themselves to you by advising you of their name and the creditor or collection agency they work for. Typically, there are three phases to the collection process:

Phase 1. Typically, creditors keep all collections in-house for about 180 days, which is generally when the account will charge off. Therefore, during this time you will be dealing directly with the creditors. Usually this is the perfect window of opportunity to negotiate a reduction in interest or a settlement as seen in Chapters 6 and 7. Early on in the delinquency, the creditor will negotiate a hardship program with you and as the debt approaches charge-off, the creditor will generally negotiate a 30% to 50% settlement. The creditor is attempting to prevent this account from charging off and going to a third-party collector where they will pay a contingency fee upwards of 40% of the amount collected or worse yet being sold for 1-20 cents on the dollar.

Phase 2. The original creditor is still the owner of the account but transfers the account to an outside collection agency or attorney, and pays them a contingency for collections provided they collect money on the account. However, if they are not successful in collecting money, they will be paid nothing for their efforts. This is the point where the collection activity becomes very aggressive because the third-party agency wants to be paid for their collection efforts. This means it is a great time to negotiate a settlement, and so is not the time to agree to payment in full or lowering your interest rates.

Phase 3. This is when the original creditor sells your account to a debt buyer or collection agency for pennies on the dollar. The debt buyer is now the creditor and has the same ability to collect on the account as the original creditor did. The original creditor sells the account to mitigate their losses. The new creditor will become very aggressive to collect this account and is open to settlement negotiations.

HANDLING DEBT COLLECTION CORRESPONDENCE

If you are contacted in writing from a third-party collection agency or collection attorney, the first letter must provide you with a consumer rights notice. The following is an example of a consumer rights notice:

"ABC Collection, LLC is a debt collection agency. This is an attempt to collect a debt and any information obtained will be used for that purpose. Unless you notify this office within 30 days after receiving this notice that you dispute the validity of this debt or any portion thereof, this office will assume the debt valid. If you notify this office in writing within 30 days from receiving this notice that you dispute the validity of this debt or any portion thereof, this office will obtain verification of the debt or obtain a copy of the judgment and mail a copy of such judgment or verification to you. If you request this office in writing within 30 days after receiving this notice, this office will provide you with the name and address of the original creditor, if different from the current creditor. If your financial institution rejects and returns your payment for any reason, a service fee—the maximum allowed by your state's statutory laws—may be added to your account balance."

If your initial contact is by phone, the collection agency must send a written notice to you within five days of that call. Additionally, the consumer rights notice must only advise you that the collection agency has been retained to assist the creditor in collecting the debt. The letter must provide you with the creditor's name and claim amount due. A third-party agency cannot demand payment during the first 30 days whether in writing or via phone, as it is deemed overshadowing under the Fair Debt Collection Act (FDCPA), which is against the law. Also, if you dispute the validity of the debt in its entirety, the collection agency cannot demand payment until they prove the claim is due and owed by you.

Therefore, when you are contacted by a third-party (outside agency) collector you need to dispute the validity of the debt and ask for verification of the debt to ensure the debt they are collecting on belongs to you. To request verification and validation of the account and balance due you must notify the collection agency in writing within 30 days of the date of the notice that you dispute the validity of the debt in its entirety. You need to request the name of the original creditor, the original balance due, the current interest rate, and an itemized listing of any and all additional fees that have been added to the original balance, and a copy of the written agreement allowing such fees to be added. Doing this will give you additional time to make a plan to get the account paid but also assure you that the debt they are collecting on belongs to you and that the amount claimed due is not fraudulently inflated. The collection agency should reply in writing with these specifics. In some cases, however, the collection agency fails to prove their claim or even inflates the balances (which is illegal). If the collection agency cannot prove their claim, they cannot collect on that claim until they can prove to the consumer that the claim is due.

Keep in mind if you are speaking with the in-house collection department of the creditor, they will likely have a few years' worth of statements and documentation regarding the balance they are collecting on.

HANDLING COLLECTION ATTORNEY CORRESPONDENCE

More and more creditors are turning their account over to attorneys for collection in lieu of regular collection agencies. This does not mean you are being sued nor does it mean you are going to be sued. In order to be sued the attorney must first file an action with the court (Summons and Complaint) and a copy of this filing along with instructions advising you how and where and when you must file an answer. These must be served upon you by a process server, certified return receipt mail, or another verified service. Once that is completed there must be a court proceeding to determine the outcome of the suit. In the event you do not respond accordingly, a default judgment may be entered against you.

Creditors are turning to collection attorneys because a letter from a law firm sounds more official and is more likely to scare a person into paying the bill. But the cold hard facts are whether or not the creditor decides to take you to court to collect the money due is an economic decision. That decision is based on the amount that is due, how long the account has been delinquent, cost of the trial, and whether or not a win on the creditor's part is going to effectuate collections. Because remember, once the creditor obtains the judgment against the debtor (consumer), they still have to collect that judgment through liens, levies, and/or wage garnishment, which all have to be done though court proceedings and the debtor has the right to defend each of those proceedings brought against them. Simply put, the uncertainties and costs associated with a lawsuit are not always in the creditor's best interest, which increases the likelihood of you settling your account for a fair price.

Collection attorneys must abide by the same FDCPA, FCRA, and FTC laws as a third-party collection agency. In fact, they are more likely to comply, due to the possibility of being sanctioned through the attorneys' ethics committee or worse, losing their ability to practice law. Therefore, you should treat a correspondence from an attorney the same as you would one from a collection agency.

HANDLING A DEBT BUYER CORRESPONDENCE

When receiving a correspondence from a debt buyer, the initial correspondence will advise you that you are now the owner of the debt as well as provide you with your consumer rights notice. You should treat this correspondence the same way you would that of a collection agency. More importantly, when a debt buyer purchases debt, they rarely receive supporting documentation and validity of the debt. They generally receive a spreadsheet with the debtor's name and social security number, the amount of the debt, the date the account went delinquent, the date of charge-off, and the interest rate. What this means for you is that once you dispute the validity of the debt, they have to contact the original creditor and hope that the proper documentation necessary to support their claim against you still exists. This can be a time-consuming event taking up to 60 days before they receive any information from the original creditor. If the creditors have the information to provide, they generally do so in 45 to 60 days. In many cases the original creditor does not have the documentation to provide to the debt buyer, which means by law the debt buyer cannot pursue collection activity against you.

PSYCHOLOGY OF DEBT COLLECTORS

Debt collectors often act as authority figures, because most of us tend to respect authority. Their stern and seemingly threatening comments may make you very upset or even frighten you, leading you to say the wrong thing or to give in to the creditor's demands. Do *not* be intimidated by collectors. Creditors and collection agencies send their collection representatives through extensive training to ask leading questions and to make statements that frighten most people into paying exactly what the bill collector is demanding.

Below are examples of what a collector may say:

> ➤ If your account is not brought to a current status, we will report this account to the credit bureaus.

> ➤ If you do not bring this account current, we will forward this to our legal department.

> ➤ Failure to make payment will result in a lawsuit being filed against you.

> ➤ Our policy is not to settle accounts for less than the full balance.

> ➤ You have an obligation to pay this account in full and we will take whatever legal measures necessary to collect payment in full.

These statements may compel you to respond to the collector demands and agree to the terms that they are setting. Do not give in to their demands and remember there is absolutely no law in any state that requires you to engage a collector or stay on the telephone and subject yourself to the collector's demands and/or threats.

One thing that we want to make very *clear*—don't hide from your debts; you will be much better off if you answer the calls, are upfront with them, and respond to their correspondence. You can, however, delay paying the bill by negotiations and getting the terms that best fit into your financial plan.

GUIDE TO COLLECTION CALLS

We have put together a customer reference guide to assist in handling creditor calls, as receiving excessive calls daily from creditors can be very stressful and frustrating. By following the outlined suggestions, you may be able to reduce your stress and frustration associated with these calls.

Identify who you are receiving calls from. Information you need to obtain when a bill collector calls includes the following:

1. Creditor's name

2. Caller's name

3. Telephone number of the person calling

4. The name of the company the collector is calling from

Keep track of all collection calls coming in and write this information down and keep it in your Call Log (found in the appendix). Keeping a log will help you track who is contacting you.

Determine if the calls have been excessive. As a rule, each creditor may attempt to contact you one to four times per day during the first two to 4 months of delinquency. This is not usually constant activity but tends to occur randomly week by week. If you have seven creditors, this might means you are receiving 7-28 calls a day for one week and 14-56 the next. (Don't worry, this doesn't keep up forever.) Oftentimes calls from original creditors increase immediately before being turned over to a collection agency.

Verbally request the creditor to stop calling. In many cases, simply requesting that a creditor stop calling you can reduce the number of calls you receive. This is especially true regarding calls at work. If you are receiving a creditor call at work and it is unacceptable to you, you should demand the creditor not contact you. The FDCPA mandates that the collector must cease communication at work once they are instructed to do so. Follow up this verbal request with a written request and keep a copy of the letter on file and date it was sent.

Written request to cease verbal communication. If the calls continue at a high rate and are of a harassing nature, you may need to send a request in writing to the creditor advising them to cease and desist communication; see sample letter in the appendix.

When speaking with a collector, it is very important that you immediately take control of the conversation. Now it's important for you to understand why the collector is calling you, first they want to verify they have your correct mailing address, phone number and social security number. Should they report the delinquency to the credit bureaus and/or move forward with sending your account to a third party collection agency, attorney and/or filing a lawsuit. Collection calls are fact finding missions. These calls will assist the creditors when your account is charging off. Based on the information they obtain from you and your credit bureaus they will either send your account to a third party collection agency or attorney for further collections, sell your debt to a debt buyer or place it in their legal department for further review and possible lawsuit.

Keep in mind your credit bureau report (credit report) will only show your creditor/collectors your current trend in paying all creditor accounts that you have. It does not provide them with your income level, your employer, or any other personal information. Therefore, it's important to control the level of information that you provide them and be consistent with that information as all calls are monitored and recorded for accuracy. For examples of effective call scripts to use when speaking with a creditor see the call scripts in the appendix.

You: Hello.

Collector: This is Joe Collector with ABC Creditor. May I speak with John Consumer.

You: This is he.

Collector: I need to speak with you about your account with Original Creditor for account verification please, verify your social security number and mailing address.

You: I don't feel comfortable with giving my personal information to someone who called me. You called me, so you should have my information available.

Collector: I'm sorry, in order for me to discuss your account with you I must receive verification.

You: I understand, however, you called me, so you should have my information available. May I get your name and phone number and the name of the company you are calling from and the account number your call is regarding?

Collector: My name is Joe Collector. I am calling with ABC Creditor. My phone number is 555-555-1212. Before I can give you your account information, I need you to verify your information.

> ***Note:*** *It is important that you get the information of the debt collector calling. If they are unwilling to give you this information, then you may question the intent of the call and purpose for the call.*

You: As I said before, Joe, you called me, therefore, you should have my information. I am not going to verify anything because I do not know who you are or what you are calling in regards to. If you cannot tell me why you called, we have nothing to discuss—goodbye.

If the collector gives you the information and the information given is correct then you can verify your information and move on with the call script as follows. If the collector does not comply, simply say "good bye" and hang up.

Collector: The collector will respond in one of three ways:

1. Please take my number and return the call.

2. We are showing that your account is past due and would like to bring the account current today with a payment in the amount of X. Will you be able to make that payment by phone today?

3. The collector will be aggressive with you and demand the information.

You: Depending on the collector's response, you will respond as follows:

1. Thank you.

2. Unfortunately, I'm unable to make a payment at this time; and I am hoping to bring resolution to this matter as soon as possible. I understand you want me to make a payment right now, but that just isn't possible. I have your phone number and will call you if my situation changes. Thank you.

3. If the collector starts harassing you and giving you a hard time, simply say goodbye and hang up.

CEASE AND DESIST

If a collection agency is continually calling you non-stop, you can send them a "cease and desist" letter. See the appendix for a sample cease and desist letter.

CIVIL LIABILITY

When debt collectors break the law, they can be sued for failing to comply with the federal and state rules and forced to pay as follows:

➤ The actual damage sustained

➤ Additional damages up to $1,000 (for each individual)

➤ The lesser of $500,000 or 1% of the debt collector's net worth (in a class action suit)

If you believe that a debt collection agency has violated any of these laws while collecting a debt from you, you should report the inappropriate behavior to your state Attorney Generals and the Federal Trade Commission (FTC) at:

Attorney General: www.naag.org/attorneys_general

FTC: www.ftc.gov or 877-FTC-HELP

CHAPTER 6

NEGOTIATING YOUR HARDSHIP, REDUCING YOUR INTEREST RATES, AND SCHEDULING PAYMENT PLANS

NEGOTIATING YOUR DEBT HARDSHIP

Up until fairly recently, common industry practice was that you needed to be late with your payments before you could get a credit card modification. However, today that has changed. Now the mentality of creditors has changed dramatically. For example, recently Bank of America stated that they expected to complete over 1.2 million credit card modifications, which is a 20% increase from 2008. Also, JP Morgan Chase has recently expanded eligibility for its repayment programs to include borrowers who may be in the earlier stages of delinquency on their accounts.

While negotiations and changes to credit card agreements are becoming more common, you still can't say that just anyone can rewrite the terms of their card agreements. Modifications are still reserved for those families and individuals who are in true financial distress.

Most consumers make every effort possible by trying to make the minimum payment on their credit cards and other bills, yet unfortunately find that they cannot afford the minimum monthly payments. If this is your problem you need to contact your creditors and negotiate a smaller minimum monthly payment. We recommend that you request a balance liquidation plan (BLP). This is when the creditor reduces your interest rate to a fixed rate of to 0% to 9% and sets you up on a 36-to-60-month repayment term. Before contacting your creditors to negotiate your interest and repayment terms, the first thing you will want to do is access a recent, free copy of your credit report. You can get a free copy of your credit report at www.annualcreditreport.com.

Before negotiating any debts, you should have a clear understanding of your financial plan, your budget, and your creditworthiness. We recommend that you purchase your credit/FICO score. This is a snapshot of your overall credit. Scores above 720 are excellent; scores below 600 are poor.

Remember that a credit card company knows almost everything about your financial picture and condition, including your credit scores, spending habits, and income. So, you probably will not have success in negotiating an adjustment if you do not have a hardship and you are only requesting adjustments to save a few bucks per month.

HOW CREDIT CARD ISSUERS NEGOTIATE

Few creditors are willing to give details on their process, or even confirm that they negotiate, but some have provided details. One bank has stated that they review and examine a number of different factors, including the borrower's spending habits, finances, and overall history when the customer calls. For example, whether the customer has been profitable to the bank or has been part of a good account with the lender is a key factor. Some factors that creditors examine before negotiating fees or rates include the following:

➢ Does the cardholder have a balance on their account?

➢ Does the cardholder have a high volume of transactions?

➢ Does the cardholder have balance transfers of cash advances?

➢ Is the credit card account a revolving account?

➢ Is the credit card account mature? (Has the cardholder made at least four to six payments?)

The creditor is trying to decide if they can lower a customer's interest rate or fees, and they conduct these reviews on a case-by-case basis. Also, if banks do lower rates, increase credit lines, or negotiate fees, the bank needs to ensure they are still profitable.

A good history and paying habits will help your cause. If you have not had good paying habits, it may be harder to get the creditor to provide you relief and negotiate with you. While people do negotiate their credit card interest rates, fees, and limits themselves, it can be a bit stressful and difficult process for some.

Consumer Credit Counseling Service (CCCS) has indicated that for an interest rate or penalty to be changed or have a credit card fee waived, banks today are more willing to work with consumers. In addition to negotiating your credit card penalties and fees, many creditors are now offering consumers short-term programs that will reduce the payment and interest rate for a period of time, usually 6 months to one year, to help the consumer get back on solid financial ground. However, this is a temporary fix and is much better for the lender than you.

NEGOTIATION TACTICS

First, be candid and open. Sum up your situation for the creditor. You need to explain that your financial situation has changed, but stress that you still want to honor your commitment to pay your bills. You can either ask what they can offer you, or better yet propose your own plan. During the negotiations they may say yes, no, or they may refer you to another department.

We believe your best option is to focus on a BLP and getting a lower interest rate and a fixed 60-month payment plan that will pay off your principal and interest. Also, be sure there is no penalty for early payment of the principal balance.

Never be afraid to negotiate strongly and haggle very much as if you would buying a car or house. Just as in most negotiations, you should very rarely accept the first offer presented to you.

One common question is should you mention bankruptcy to them. If this is an option you're seriously considering doing, then absolutely yes, you need to say it to them.

NEGOTIATION PROCESS

Preparation is important in any negotiation process and it is especially important in negotiating your debt. Remember, your creditors already have a snapshot of your financial profile and spending habits. To negotiate your hardship plan, follow these four steps:

Step 1. Calculate your debt-to-income ratio (DIR). This is a calculation lenders use to determine your ability to pay back your creditors. To find this percentage, divide the sum of your monthly bills by your total gross income each month. Lenders will not offer hardship programs if you show that you currently have the ability to repay your loans. A DIR above 50% shows a clear economic hardship. However, you must show the creditor that there is a benefit to enrolling you into a hardship program and that you can afford to meet your new payment obligations on a monthly basis long term.

Step 2. Collect all documents relating to your economic hardship. These can include unemployment stubs, disability award letters, medical/doctor letters, and bankruptcy papers. You may need these to argue your case when you open negotiations.

Step 3. Contact your creditor and explain to them that you are having a hardship and need to speak with someone about your account. The customer service agent may be able to assist you or may transfer you to a specialist. Be specific about what you are looking for. Again, we recommend that you request a BLP (Balance Liquidation Plan) and request your interest rate to be reduced to a fixed rate of 0% to 9% and set up on a 60-month repayment term. Before you accept the creditor's plan, make sure it fits into your budget long term.

Step 4. Get the final hardship plan in writing. This should cover the fact that your account has a fixed interest rate of X and your new monthly payment of X has a due date of 00/00/0000. Additionally, it should state that late fees and over limit will be waived. Accordingly, it will have a stipulation regarding default. Review all terms and make sure the plan is financially beneficial for you. Only sign the document after you review it and determine that this is the right plan for you.

INFORMATION ON CREDIT CARD HARDSHIP PROGRAMS

Below you will find information regarding some creditor hardship programs as well as phone numbers to their loss-mitigation departments.

American Express. American Express has a hardship program that is very effective at eliminating debt, as it can reduce your monthly payment by as much as 40%. However, that is more for extreme hardship cases. Normally, the reduction in your monthly credit card bills will be closer to 10% to 25%, according to spokespeople from American Express. They may reduce your monthly payment and cancel penalties and fees. They also will offer longer-term solutions such as debt management plans. If you need help or are interested in the American Express assistance program, call 800-253-1709 to speak with a service representative.

Bank of America. Credit card debt relief options include eliminating fees, lowering the interest rate you pay, starting you on a debt management plan, or reducing your monthly payment. You can contact Bank of America at 800-500-5306 to learn more about their credit card hardship programs and assistance available.

Capital One. They offer struggling consumers negotiated payment plans, late fee and other waivers, a reduction in your APR, and more. Get more information on Capital One credit card assistance plans at 866-929-5303. Also, locate an example of how real customers are receiving debt assistance from Capital One.

Chase. Chase will suspend future late and over-limit fees, plus they can reduce your credit card interest rates, and even extend repayment terms. To contact Chase for more information on hardship programs, call the toll free number on your card. Also, find some of the current deals that Chase is offering for hardship customers.

Citibank. Citibank offers a credit card hardship program as well. Assistance provided can include temporary credit card debt forbearance, debt consolidation, loan workouts, debt settlement plans, and interest rate reductions. To find out more on the Citibank Credit Card Hardship Program, call Citibank at 866-936-4814.

Discover Card. Discover credit cardholders who are experiencing a financial emergency or severe hardships may be able to receive a temporary single-digit APR. Another resource they offer is debt management plans, which may prove to be your best option in some situations. If you are a Discover Card member, you can call 866-567-1660 for more information on their debt help programs.

Note: Discover Card has a reputation of being one of the credit card issuers that is not as forthcoming with offering assistance. So, if you get any cooperation or offers from them, it is recommended to take it!

HSBC credit card hardship programs. HSBC is also trying to help thousands of consumers deal with their debt by offering them hardship programs. They are yet another bank that has decided it is better to work with customers for partly their own reasons. They have decided it is better to get customers to pay some of their credit card bills rather than see the customer default on their debts, or file bankruptcy, or otherwise not pay HSBC anything.

HSBC is also pushing a hardship program to aggressively provide support to customers who are struggling with paying their credit card bills and debts. Call customer service at 888-385-8916 for more on HSBC's programs.

GE Money Bank. Hardship programs are also offered by GE Money Bank. You can contact them at 866-396-8254 to apply or get additional information on your options. Also, read examples of how account holders are settling their credit card debt with GE Money Bank.

CHAPTER 7

DO-IT-YOURSELF DEBT SETTLEMENT

ARE YOU A CANDIDATE FOR DEBT SETTLEMENT?

Before you can prepare yourself for debt settlement, you have to know if you are a candidate for debt settlement. To do so, answer the following questions:

1. How much do you owe in credit card debt?

    a. Do you have any other unsecured debt such as past-due medical bills, repossessions or personal loans?

2. Have you had any slow or late payments in the last 12 months?

3. Is this debt something you have been struggling with for some time now?

4. Are you finding it increasingly difficult to make your minimum monthly payments and still afford your necessary living expenses?

    a. Your Answer: must be YES to qualify

5. Are you currently employed or self-employed?

      a.   Your Answer: must be YES to qualify

6.   Can you set aside $X for your debt settlement? X equals your to-
tal amount of unsecured debt multiplied by 45% and divided by
number months that you would like to be debt-free.

      a.   Example: credit card debt $15,000 x 45% = 6,750/24
months = $281.25

Your Answer: Must be YES to qualify

HOW WERE YOUR CREDIT CARDS USED?

Usage of your credit cards will play a big role when the creditors are evaluating your account for settlement. Creditors will look at the usage of
each card and determine if they will negotiate with you and if so, how
much that they are willing to negotiate. Therefore, it is vital that you know
how the cards were used. The following scenarios will affect how the
creditor will negotiate with you:

➤ Have you made at least three payments on the card(s) you are settling?

    ○   If no, you can expect to settle at a higher rate or possibly
be denied the settlement option altogether.

➤ Have you transferred other card balances to the card(s) you are
settling?

    ○   If yes, you can expect to settle at a higher rate.

➤ Have you taken cash advances on the card(s) you are settling?

    ○   If yes, you can expect to settle at a higher rate.

➤ Have you used the card heavily in the last 3 months?

    ○   If yes, you can expect to settle at a higher rate or possibly
be denied settlement options altogether.

DOES YOUR DEBT QUALIFY FOR SETTLEMENT?

Only unsecured debts will qualify for debt settlement. These debts are not
secured by real assets like homes or automobiles. Below are examples of dif-

ferent types of unsecured and secured debts.

Debt types that can qualify for settlement are:

- ➢ Credit cards

- ➢ Medical bills

- ➢ Unsecured loans

- ➢ Unsecured personal loans

- ➢ Unsecured personal lines of credit

- ➢ Collections, autos in repossession

Debt types that cannot qualify for settlement are:

- ➢ Home loans/mortgages

- ➢ Automobile loans

- ➢ Student loans

- ➢ Government loans

- ➢ Lawsuits, IRS debt / taxes

- ➢ Secured debts. Examples: Honda motorcycle/lawn machines, Suzuki motorcycle, furniture, etc.

- ➢ Starr, NEX, and AAFES military cards

THE DEBT SETTLEMENT PROCESS

Most do-it-yourself debt settlement plans fail because people do not properly prepare and set aside funds to settle their accounts. The average debt settlement plan takes between 12 and 36 months to complete depending on the amount of debt and number of creditors. The key variable in determining how long it will take you to complete your plan is determining your debt-to-income ratio.

Settlement offers will depend on the account delinquency and the creditor's settlement criteria. Typically, creditors will reduce accounts based on your hardship and the number of days the account is delinquent. The following chart is an example of estimated settlements that you can expect:

Days Delinquent	Settlement Offers
30-75	75% to 90%
76-120	45% to 65%
121-179	30% to 60%

The settlement offer that you receive will largely depend on your hardship, your ability to negotiate, and if you are paying a lump sum or if you need to make payments.

In order to put yourself in the best position for the lowest settlement offer you must prepare yourself and your case that you will be presenting to the creditor. Your case will explain to the creditor why you should be the benefactor of a settlement. The following are key steps that you must take in the preparation of your debt settlement plan:

➢ Prepare your financial plan and budget.

➢ Determine the cause of your financial hardship and write it down; be as detailed as possible. The reason this is important is your creditor will ask you what caused your financial hardship. Examples of valid hardships are:

   o Divorce

   o Job loss

   o Loss of income

   o Demotions

   o Illness in family

   o Death in family

   o Credit card minimum payments increasing

   o Supporting parents

   o Failing business

   o Child in legal trouble

Be prepared to back up your hardship with supporting documents. Anything that you have to substantiate your hardship will assist you in obtaining the lowest available settlement.

➢ Understand you are attempting to settle the account(s) for X amount and that you can reasonably manage and work this amount into your financial plan and budget.

   o Determine how many accounts you need to settle and calculate the total due for those accounts.

   o Set up a special-purpose account. This is an account where you will set aside funds to pay the creditors once you have reached a settlement.

   o Calculate how much money you will need to settle these accounts. Use a formula of 45% of the current balance. This is a safe percentage to use since some creditors will settle around 30% and others will settle around 55%.

      ▪ Example: If you have five credit cards totaling $25,000.00, you will need to set aside $11,250.00 to settle these accounts.

   o Now determine how much money you can safely set aside each month to reach your goal of $11,250.00. Use the chart below to determine the number of months that you require to save the necessary funds needed to settle your accounts. If at all possible, do not exceed the maximum allotted time below

Debt Amount	Maximum Time	Monthly Savings
$7,500-$9,999	30 Months	$141.00 - $206.00
$10,000-$14,999	36 Months	$165.00 - $225.00
$15,000-$29,999	42 Months	$188.00 – 312.00
$30,000-Plus	48 Months	$234.00-Plus

Note: Remember, the creditor can and may pursue legal action against you. So, it is very important that you set aside as much money as you can as quickly as possible to effectuate a settlement. The longer it takes you save money to obtain a settlement, the greater your risk is of the creditor taking legal action. The above chart is simply a guide—the quicker you save, the quicker you will be debt-free.

> ➤ Keep a file of all your statements and letters from collection agencies. This will assist you when you are ready to contact the creditor to make a settlement offer.

STARTING THE NEGOTIATIONS

If you are considering debt settlement, your account(s) need to be at least 90 days or more delinquent before creditors will want to negotiate any significant settlement with you. You will receive your best settlement offers right before or at "charge off," which is generally 180 days delinquent.

Now your account is at least 90 days plus delinquent and you have sufficient funds available to make a settlement offer on your account. Call the customer service department at the 1-800 telephone numbers on your statements or on letters that you have received. Inform the person you are speaking with of your hardship. Keep it simple and direct. You should be aware that they are taking notes, which will be made part of your account records permanently. If you find the collector is rude and unwilling to help you, do not argue and never use profane language. Ask to speak to a supervisor or department manager and proceed when that person is on the phone. Express your interest in settling the account, but do not make a proposal. If your account is eligible for settlement, they will propose an offer to you immediately.

Your balance will have increased due to the finance charges and late fees that your account has accrued while being delinquent. Generally, once the account charges off you will not incur additional fees unless you are sued. Then you may be responsible for court costs and other legal fees associated with the lawsuit.

WHAT TO EXPECT FROM THE CREDITOR

The creditor's first offer may be to reduce or eliminate interest and to set you up on a hardship plan that will re-age your account and bring it to a current status. This is not a good offer for you—do not be intimidated; you are not obligated to take their offer. You will want to refuse this offer and explain that you would like to settle the account. Depending on the delinquency of the account, the creditor may offer a 50% to 75% settlement. Again, do not be intimated—you can counter with a settlement offer of 30% of the balance due. If they refuse the offer today, chances are they will accept or make a better offer later. Remember, the creditor's intentions are to collect as much as possible as quickly as possible. The longer a collector spends on a particular account the more money the creditor loses.

The truth of the matter is the creditor will make an economic decision to mitigate their losses and either except your offer at a later date opposed to sending the account to a collection agency or attorney where they will incur a collection fee upwards of 40% of the amount collected. Also, the creditor must weigh the possibility of you filing for bankruptcy, in which case, they could get nothing. It's up to you to keep the creditor guessing by negotiating firmly and if bankruptcy is a possibility, let them know.

REFUSING A PROPOSAL

If you find the offer is not acceptable or in your best interest, simply inform the collector that you need to see if their offer fits into your budget and advise them that you will contact them in a few days. Make sure that you have the representative's first and last name, the direct telephone number, fax number, and mailing address. Keep in mind that 30% to 50% of the original balance is a very good settlement offer, and it does fit into your estimated settlement budget of 45%, so you should consider accepting the offer.

> **Note:** Most professionals are settling accounts for their clients at 32% to 45% on the dollar while charging their clients 15% of the total debt being placed for settlement.

MAKING A COUNTER PROPOSAL

From your previous call with the creditor you have obtained phone and fax numbers along with the mailing address of the collector. Therefore, you can contact the collector and submit a verbal proposal and follow that up in writing by faxing and/or mailing a copy of your proposal to the collector. When you are making a proposal, be sure that you are making a realistic proposal, which is 30% to 50% of the current balance. An unrealistic proposal is 10%. Making an unrealistic proposal could jeopardize your future negotiations.

Once you have negotiated an acceptable percentage to pay, you now want to negotiate a time frame to pay. Depending on the amount of funds you have accumulated, you may want to make a lump sum payment or negotiate a payout between 3 and 12 months. If you have another account to settle, this will allow you to begin negotiations on it. Be sure to stay within your budget at all times during your negotiations.

ACCEPTANCE OF A SETTLEMENT OFFER

Once you have agreed on an acceptable settlement, you must instruct the collector to provide you with written confirmation of the offer before you remit any money. Do *not* under any circumstances make a payment by phone until you have received a written settlement offer from the collector agreeing to all the settlement terms that were negotiated. In the terms of the agreement the collectors may include payment to be made via "check-by-phone"; this is standard procedure and is acceptable once you have the signed agreement. If you wish, you can provide the creditor with your own settlement agreement. An example of this agreement can be found in the appendix.

NEGOTIATING CREDIT RATING

Generally, when a debt is settled the creditor will report it as "Satisfied" or "Settled," and this may have a negative effect on your credit score.

This is the final step in the negotiation process. However, this is a very important step—if you can, you should attempt to negotiate for either "Paid as Agreed" or "Paid as Agreed Account Closed."

CHAPTER 8

FINDING OR GENERATING ADDITIONAL INCOME

CREATING ADDITIONAL INCOME

We've all heard the saying "money makes the world go around," but for most Americans the lack of money or more specifically *debt* can make the world come to a complete standstill.

When you are in debt and struggling to get out, anything you can do to generate additional income will go a long way towards eliminating your debt, especially if you are looking to reduce and eliminate the debt quickly. Statistics show that the average family could avoid bankruptcy with just an extra $150 per week. The question now becomes how are you going to generate this extra income and how much time do you have available after working your regular job and setting time aside for your family to earn additional money.

Most people already work full-time and often put in more than 40 hours per week at their workplace. Not surprisingly, considering a second job or a part-time job sounds like more of a sacrifice than you can or maybe are willing to make—or maybe you just think we are crazy for suggesting it. We assure you, this sacrifice will be well worth it when you weigh the pros and cons of additional money or continuing to struggle with your debt.

TAX REFUNDS

According to the Internal Revenue Service (IRS), the average tax refund mailed in 2008 was about $2,500. This means millions people across the country are giving our government an interest-free loan. If you are one of the millions of Americans that are receiving a refund check each year, you need better financial planning. The reason you are receiving a refund is because your W-4 withholding is not filled out correctly and you are paying too much in your taxes. You may love getting that big refund check, but, regardless how good it feels, it simply is not wise. Instead of giving the government an interest-free loan, a more prudent decision would be to keep your money, so you can apply it towards paying off your bills, put it into savings, or simply spend it wisely.

To adjust your W-4, go to your Human Resource or Payroll department and advise them that you want to take out less tax from your paycheck. On your next payday, you will notice your paycheck is larger. Use the extra money to pay down your debt. Be sure that when you make this adjustment you keep track of the amount of taxes you are paying, because you don't want to pay too little in taxes and end up owing money to the IRS when April 15 comes rolling around. However, if you owe a small amount, it's much better than receiving a refund—as it means you had more cash to put towards bills or savings than the previous years.

BUSINESS OPPORTUNITIES

Regardless of the economy, there is always a need for goods and services. Now may be the perfect time to consider starting a small, home-based business. People from all walks of life across the country are starting their own small business—in fact, a new, home-based business starts every six seconds in America! Using your home, garage, or apartment is one of the best ways to launch your new business. One of the most appealing things about a home-based business is you can do it part time while working your regular job.

We are firm believers that in life if you think it, you can make it happen and if you want it, you can have it—through hard work and perseverance. After all, we do live in an abundant society and anything is possible. With that, we do not want to send the wrong message; just because you start your own business, it does not guarantee that you will earn a six-figure income and/or be able to quit your regular job.

However, if you start a business and provide a much-needed service or goods, the likelihood of your success will be greatly improved.

THE INTERNET

If you are a web and computer-savvy person, we suggest you harness the power of the Internet to make some additional money—legally, of course. From eBay to taking online surveys, there are many ways to make money on the Internet these days. We believe your best option would be to choose a business that works into your lifestyle and provides a good or service that is in demand and very much needed.

CHAPTER 9

CHOOSING THE BEST DEBT ELIMINATION STRATEGY

Coming face-to-face with financial trouble may seem to be more than you can handle, at first. Fortunately, you have options. Whether you go at it alone or retain the service of a reputable company, you can get yourself started again in the right direction.

Don't make the mistake of doing nothing and understand that you have power and leverage when it comes to dealing with your creditors. Regardless of the fact that you are making the minimum payment and have fallen behind, your creditors do not want to lose your business or money.

What is the most effective method of eliminating your debt? Depending on your financial troubles, only one out the six described in this book will not be effective—and that one is doing nothing. When determining what is best for you, we suggest you first evaluate your risk factors and understand that anything short of paying off your debt in full may have a negative impact on your credit score and could involve a creditor filing suit against you.

The first thing you need to do is determine how much debt you have—not knowing how much debt you have is sort of like refusing to step on the scale. You can fool yourself for a little while, juggling bills and expenses, but eventually, it's going to catch up to you. Harvard law professor Elizabeth

Warren, the country's leading bankruptcy researcher, says in her book *The Two Income Trap* that "false optimism" is the single greatest danger for families in financial distress. Consumers who refuse to face the facts, so to speak, are likely to get sucked into high interest loans, scams, and so on. In 2010, we had two clients who lost $7,500 each to debt settlement scams. They both came to us and we couldn't get them into a program that they could afford to pay off their debt and they ended up filing bankruptcy, which they were trying to avoid. If they had tried to find a legitimate solution sooner, they may have had better options. Of course, they were the inspiration behind writing this book. Whatever you do—do not wait until it's too late!

Prepare your financial plan, choose your debt elimination or reduction strategy, and remain disciplined to that strategy—stay the course and you will achieve your goal of financial freedom. Remember, regardless of your choice, this will be a challenging process. Be honest with yourself and pick the strategy that best fits your financial circumstance as well as one that you can handle mentally and it should prove to be the best choice for you.

ALTERNATIVES TO CREDIT CARDS

The best alternative to a credit card is to have no credit cards at all. However, in today's society that is a bit unrealistic, so, we would recommend having one credit card that you pay off in full every month and a Visa debit card. Make sure you set financial goals for yourself every month and only spend money that you have. Using a debit card is one of the best alternatives to a credit card. However, we recommend that you use cash in lieu of a debit or credit card; as this has proven to reduce consumer spending by 10% to 27% monthly. If you choose to use a debt card over cash for convenience purposes, be sure to save your receipts and track your daily expenses using: www.mint.com, www.gosimplifi.com, Intuit Quicken, or Microsoft Money. Any of these software programs can help you keep track of your daily expenses to make sure that you are not over spending.

ACCELERATED DEBT ELIMINATION PLAN (ADEP)

If you have the ability to make your monthly minimum payments and are doing so, we recommend that you look into an ADEP.

BALANCE LIQUIDATION PLAN (BLP)

If you have high interest rates and you are starting to pay your creditors past the due date or you are juggling your payments, a BLP may be a very good option for you.

The bank will decide to either eliminate or lower your interest rate. In addition, they will oftentimes agree to stop charging you fees, including over-limit charges or late fees. Many banks will work out a 36-60 month repayment plan with you.

❖ Your credit score will be negatively impacted because you will be closing the account and the credit debt utilization will increase. But this is temporary.

If you maintain your new monthly payments, your credit score will recover and you will be out of debt within 36 to 60 months depending on the hardship negotiated with the creditors.

CONSUMER CREDIT COUNSELING (CCC)

CCC is growing in popularity as approximately 9 million consumers seek help from CCC agencies yearly. The typical person entering into a CCC debt management plan earns about $30,000 per year and has about $16,000 in credit card debt. An effective CCC program will have you out of debt within 36 to 60 months. Pros and cons with CCC are listed below.

Pros	Cons
➢ One monthly payment	➢ Taking client's money and not paying their bills
➢ Lower interest rate	➢ Charging unreasonably high startup/monthly fees
➢ No negative impact on credit score	➢ Not fully disclosing CCC fees and application of creditor payments

DEBT SETTLEMENT

Debt settlement is an extreme measure and should only be considered if you cannot afford an ADEP or the monthly payments of a BLP or debt management plan offered through a CCC. Debt settlement is a legal and effective strategy to reduce and eliminate your debt. The average debt settlement program takes 36 months to complete depending on the amount of debt that you have and your ability to set aside funds for lump-sum settlements.

Debt settlement is a great strategy if you have access to some money or are disciplined and have the ability to set aside funds, so you can negotiate a settlement of your creditors and repay a fraction of what you owe. The following are some of the negative implications associated with debt settlement:

❖ This will lower your credit score similar to if the debt were written off by the credit card company.

❖ Having to deal with collection calls.

❖ A creditor could file a lawsuit against you.

> ➤ You can still negotiate a settlement after a lawsuit has been filed.

❖ Tax consequences to debt settlement. Oftentimes if a creditor forgives more than $600 worth of the principal on your credit card debt, it will report the amount that is forgiven to the IRS via a 1099-C form. Here's an illustration of how this may work: If a card issuer negotiates with you and you agree to make a lump-sum payment to get out of credit card debt—for example, you pay a $2,500 payment to settle a $4,500 credit card bill—you will probably have to pay income tax on an additional $2,000 next year. But another option is if the credit card company eliminates fees or interest that is due, or if they agree to lower your interest rate, then there are no tax consequences.

> ➤ The tax liabilities are generally far less than paying the full balance.

CHAPTER 10

DEALING WITH DEPRESSION, STRESS, AND ANXIETY CAUSED BY OVERWHELMING DEBT

DEALING WITH DEPRESSION

Healing is a slow process; some days are going to be good and others bad. The most important thing is knowing that you are regaining control of your life, and the best way to do that is to maintain financial goals in a realistic time frame. If you have spare time, choose fun activities that do not require spending a lot of money. Sometimes going for hikes or just being outdoors is a very effective way to begin the healing process. Being with friends and family is perhaps the best way to start smiling again. Or maybe working out will do the trick for you. Spend time prioritizing what is important in your life and try to place less emphasis on material things. We do, however, encourage you to treat yourself to a nice meal or go out with friends and spend a little now and then. The healing process takes time.

DEALING WITH STRESS

Stress is a normal reaction to something that is considered a challenge or threat. Everyone gets stressed at times. It is important to understand that the same situation can produce different levels of stress in different people. For example: Negotiating over a price is very stressful for some people, yet positively enjoyable for others.

Stress is also a natural part of life and is even healthy in small doses. When it builds up, however, it can start to do more harm than good.

When under stress the human body prepares for action. This preparation is often referred to as the "fight or flight" response. In the short term, the physical change it brings about makes a person stronger and more alert. This natural response is designed to help a person get out of trouble. Other times it can help get someone through a job, or adjust to a major change, like the arrival of a new child. As debt builds up, it's easy to feel stressed out. As you choose and start implementing your debt management strategy, you will notice your pain and frustration will start diminish and eventually, it will be gone altogether, along with your debt.

DEALING WITH ANXIETY

Anxiety can be tough. It often comes on fast and can sometimes be unbearable. Many people feel overwhelmed with debt, get anxious when opening their bills or looking at bank statements. Debt problems cause a lot of anxiety. Most people become so wrapped up in their own problems that they forget about everyone else. At the same time, they may begin to take out their feelings on family and friends. The result can be bad feelings between family members, along with a loss of friends. Many people have talked about hurting those closest to them; this is tough to deal with. Anxiety will limit your effectiveness at work. Over a long period, it will gradually wear you down. You will become physically weaker and begin to tire more easily. At the same time, you will find it harder to concentrate.

Stay true to your cause of improving your financial situation and don't become a victim of depression, stress, or anxiety caused by overwhelming debt.

DEBT STATISTICS

It's no wonder consumers are dealing with depression, stress, and anxiety over their debt troubles—most consumers face a multitude of debt challenges every day.

> ➢ Statistics show the average family can waste 10% of their monthly income shopping for everyday items.

- ➢ The average household in America currently has $11,000 in credit card debt.

- ➢ At 65 years old, the average American has $500 in the bank and no retirement plan other than social security.

- ➢ Most families can't afford a vacation, causing stress and poor performance on the job from a lack of ample rest and relaxation.

- ➢ Finances are the main cause of up to 75% of divorces today.

- ➢ Statistics show one in two families will encounter a lawsuit at some point costing up to $20,000. The majority of families will have a significant tax error resulting in a very costly audit.

- ➢ An identity is stolen every three seconds; the average time to resolve the issue is 600 hours (some on the job) and countless dollars.

- ➢ An average employee spends 20 hours a month on personal financial matters at work costing employers thousands per year.

- ➢ 90% of Americans are not satisfied with their current financial wellness.

- ➢ 70% of Americans are living paycheck to paycheck.

- ➢ 83% of Americans are spending more than they make.

- ➢ 95% of Americans are not prepared financially for retirement.

- ➢ 40% of Americans cannot qualify for a mortgage.

For every negative statistic, there is a positive statistic too. So, if you are part of the negative statistics above, this is the time to take control of your financial destiny and begin the process of transitioning yourself from the negative to the positive.

CHAPTER 11

LAWSUITS, JUDGMENTS, WAGE GARNISHMENTS, LIENS, AND BAD CHECKS

LAWSUITS

A lawsuit begins when a complaint is filed with the court. This complaint will state that one or more plaintiffs are seeking damages or equitable relief from one or more stated defendants, and will identify the legal and factual bases for doing so. It is important that the "plaintiff selects the proper venue with the proper jurisdiction to bring their lawsuit." The clerk of a court signs a summons, which is then served by the plaintiff upon the defendant, together with a copy of the complaint. This service notifies the defendants that they are being sued and that they have a specific time limit to file a response. By providing a copy of the complaint, the service also notifies the defendants of the nature of the claims. Once the defendants are served with the summons and complaint, they have a time limit to file an answer identifying their defenses to the plaintiff's claims, including any challenges to the court's jurisdiction, and any counterclaims they wish to assert against the plaintiff.

In many courts, a lawsuit begins when one or more plaintiffs properly serve a summons and complaint upon the defendant(s). In these states, the plaintiffs need not file the complaint with the district court clerk to commence the lawsuit. As in other courts, the defendant(s) will have a specific time limit during which they may file their answer.

If the defendant chooses to file an answer within the time permitted, he/she must respond to each of the plaintiffs' allegations by admitting the allegation, denying it, or pleading a lack of sufficient information to admit or deny the allegation. At the time he/she files an answer, the defendant will also raise all "affirmative" defenses he/she may have. He/she may also assert any counterclaims for damages or equitable relief against the plaintiff, and in the case of "compulsory counterclaims," must do so or risk having the counterclaim barred in any subsequent proceeding. The defendant may also file a "third-party complaint" in which he seeks to join another party or parties in the action if he believes those parties may be liable for some or all of the plaintiff's damages. Filing an answer "joins the cause" and moves the case into the pre-trial phase.

Instead of filing an answer within the time specified in the summons, the defendant can choose to dispute the validity of the complaint by filing one or more motions to dismiss. The motion must be filed within the time period specified in the summons for an answer. If all such motions are denied by the trial court, and the defendant loses on all appeals from such denials (if that option is available), then the defendant *must* file an answer.

Usually the pleadings are drafted by a lawyer, but in many courts individuals can file papers and represent themselves, which is called appearing pro se.

TRIAL AND JUDGMENT

In general, most lawsuits filed are settled through negotiation, mediation, or arbitration and do not go to trial.

However, some lawsuits may then proceed to trial, with each side presenting witnesses and submitting evidence, at the close of which the judge or jury renders their decision. Generally speaking, the plaintiff has the burden of proof in making his/her claims, which means that it is up to him/her to produce enough evidence to persuade the judge or jury that his/her claim should succeed. The defendant may have the burden of proof on other issues, however, such as affirmative defenses.

There are numerous motions that either party can file throughout the lawsuit to terminate it "prematurely"—before submission to the judge or jury for final consideration. These motions attempt to persuade the judge, through legal argument and sometimes accompanying evidence, that because there is no reasonable way that the other party could legally win, there is no sense in continuing with the trial. Motions for summary judgment[1] for example, summary judgment can usually be brought before, after, or during the actual presentation of the case. Motions can also be brought after the close of a trial to undo a jury verdict that is contrary to law or against the weight of the evidence, or to convince the judge that he should change his decision or grant a new trial.

Also, at any time during this process from the filing of the complaint to the final judgment, the plaintiff may withdraw his/her complaint and end the whole matter, or the defendant may agree to a settlement, which involves a negotiated award followed also by the plaintiff withdrawing his/her complaint and the settlement entered into the court record.

APPEAL

After a **final** decision has been made, either party or both may appeal (In law, an **appeal** is a process for requesting a formal change to an official decision) from the judgment if they are unhappy with it (and their jurisdiction grants the ability). Even the prevailing party may appeal, if, for example, they wanted a larger award than was granted. The appellate court (an **appellate court** is any court of law that is empowered to hear an appeal of a trial court or other lower tribunal. which may be structured as an intermediate appellate court) and a higher court will then affirm the judgment, refuse to hear it (which effectively affirms), reverse, or vacate and remand, which involves sending the lawsuit back to the lower trial court to address an unresolved issue, or possibly for a whole new trial. Some lawsuits go up and down the appeals ladder repeatedly before finally being resolved.

Often individuals fail to realize that facts may not be changed in an appellate court. If a party does not present a fact at the trial court level, he or she generally cannot introduce new facts upon appeal. When the matter has finally been resolved, or the allotted time to file an appeal has expired, the matter is res judicata. The plaintiff is precluded from bringing an action resulting from the same claim again. In addition, other parties who later attempt to re-litigate a matter already ruled upon from a previous lawsuit will be estopped from doing so.

---

[1] In law, a **summary judgment** is a determination made by a court *without* a full trial. Such a judgment may be issued as to the merits of an entire case, or of specific issues in that case.

ENFORCEMENT

When a final judgment is entered, the plaintiff will likely be barred under res judicata (the Latin term for "a matter already judged") from trying to bring the same or similar claim again against that defendant, or from relitigating any of the issues, even under different legal claims or theories. This prevents a new trial of the same case with a different result, or if the plaintiff won, a repeat trial that merely multiplies the judgment against the defendant.

If the judgment is for the plaintiff, then the defendant must comply under penalty of law with the judgment, which will usually be a monetary award. If the defendant fails to pay, the court has various powers to seize any of the defendant's assets located within its jurisdiction, such as:

➢ Bank account garnishment

➢ Liens

➢ Wage garnishment

If all assets are located elsewhere, the plaintiff must file another suit in the appropriate court to seek enforcement of the other court's previous judgment. This can be a difficult task when crossing from a court in one state or nation to another, though courts tend to grant each other respect when there is not a clear legal rule to the contrary. A defendant who has no assets in any jurisdiction is said to be "judgment-proof." The term is generally a colloquialism to describe an impecunious defendant.

Indigent judgment-proof defendants are no longer imprisoned; debtor's prisons have been outlawed by statute, constitutional amendment, or international human rights treaties in the vast majority of common law jurisdictions.

WHAT TO DO IF A LAWSUIT IS FILED AGAINST YOU

➢ Hire a lawyer. If you have a good defense, you need an expert to present that defense for you. A lawyer can also advise you on the best way to deal with the debt lawsuit. He may recommend a settlement, a repayment plan, or filing bankruptcy depending on your situation. In addition to this, a lawyer can negotiate with the creditors on your behalf and appear in court for you if necessary.

➢ Respond to any summons. The amount of debt determines how you are served with a summons for a debt lawsuit. A small claims debt lawsuit can be served to you via certified or registered mail. You must respond to the summons as directed. If you fail to show up in court at the appointed date and time, the court automatically rules in favor of the creditor.

➢ Negotiate a settlement. If you know you owe money, you can contact the creditor or the debt collection agency. Some creditors are willing to take less money for an upfront payment. Other creditors may re-structure the repayment plan for the debt to make it easier for you to pay the debt in full.

HOW TO ANSWER A LAWSUIT FOR DEBT COLLECTION

The following is a summary of law contained in Codes, Statutes, and Court Cases. For those who want to do further research we have included some citations—that is, the place where the summarized information can be found.

The following may assist you if you are ever served with a lawsuit in a debt collection case, and if you want to prevent garnishment of your income and assets or a lien against your property.

Please be advised, we are not attorneys and this information is not in-tended to legal advice. All information is for educational purpose and should not be considered a substitute for actual representation by a lawyer. You should always consult or hire a lawyer before answering a lawsuit.

BASIC QUESTIONS & ANSWERS

Should I answer the Complaint? Yes, if you believe that you do not owe part or all of the amounts claimed.

Do I have to answer the Complaint? No, if you agree that you owe the amount claimed or do not wish to dispute the claim.

What happens if I do not answer the Complaint? The plaintiff will win automatically. The plaintiff will get a judgment for the amount of money the plaintiff asks for in the complaint. Even if the plaintiff wins, there are limits on what the plaintiff can do to collect. See our publication "Debtors' Rights in a Lawsuit" for details.

Can I be sued for an unpaid bill even if I have offered to make small payments on my bill or even if I have told the plaintiff I would make full payments as soon as I could? Yes. However, most creditors would rather not have to spend money on lawsuits and will enter into agreements for you to pay installments. If you can't make a payment, you should contact the creditor right away and explain what happened. If they don't hear from you, they may assume you don't intend to pay and will file a lawsuit. If they win, the costs of that suit will be added to the amount you owe. The creditor does not have to accept anything less than what you owe.

Can I be sued for money even if I cannot afford to pay the debt? Yes. Being unable to afford to pay a debt is not a defense.

Why should I file a declaration declaring my exempt assets and income? This exemptions declaration lets your creditors know that you have income and/or assets that are protected from being garnished or taken. It also lets them know that if they attempt to garnish or lien these things, you can sue them under the Fair Debt Collection Practices Act (FDCPA). Be sure to include a copy of your bank statement and any other statements showing your sources of income, but black out or cover up your account number and your social security number on those statements first. Also, if your spouse has income from a non-exempt resource, like wages, your spouse should open her or his own account and deposit the non-exempt funds there. That account will be at risk of garnishment if your spouse is named in the Complaint.

What are a Summons and Complaint? When any lawsuit is started, the person starting it must prepare a statement, telling the judge what the problem is and what he or she wants. That statement is called the Complaint, and the person starting the lawsuit is called the plaintiff. If the lawsuit is against you, you are the defendant. A copy of the Complaint must be delivered to you so that you will know about the lawsuit. You will also receive a Summons, which tells you that you have a right to disagree with the Complaint **in writing.** It also tells you the amount of time you have to answer the Complaint, and where to deliver your Answer.

If you do not tell the court in writing that you disagree with the statements in the Complaint, the judge will assume that you agree with it and will usually give the plaintiff what he or she asks for. In other words, the plaintiff wins by default, since you have not answered. If a Default Judgment is entered in the court records against you, you will not necessarily be notified if you have not answered. Once a judgment is entered against you, the plaintiff may be able to use that judgment to take money from your bank account or paycheck, or to take some of your property to pay the judgment. Therefore, it is very important that you file a **written response** within the time limit given by your summons (usually 20 days; read your Summons carefully for the deadline).

You may respond by delivering either a Notice of Appearance or an Answer to the person who signed the Summons and Complaint. A Notice of Appearance merely states that you have appeared in the lawsuit. By delivering a Notice of Appearance, you will prevent the court from entering a default judgment against you without a court hearing. **A Notice of Appearance does not explain your position in the lawsuit. This will be done when you file your Answer.** You should use the form Notice of Appearance that is attached. You should try to do both the Notice of Appearance and the Answer at the same time. If you can't, it is very important that you at least do the Notice of Appearance because if it is delivered and filed before the plaintiff goes to court, he or she must inform you of all further court hearings. A sample Notice of Appearance and a Notice of Appearance form are attached. **You should plan on delivering and filing your Answer before you go to court.** You can use the attached Answer form to fill in the necessary information. To fill it out, follow the directions below.

What is an Answer? The Answer is your written response to the statements in the Complaint. You are called the defendant.

In your Answer, you do not have to tell the entire story or make legal arguments. You do need to state whether you agree or disagree with each statement in the complaint. Your answer should be typed, but if you cannot have it typed, you can neatly hand write it, using print (not cursive writing).

Your Answer **does** need to be clear and readable, and it must say whether you agree or disagree with some or all of the statements in the Complaint, or whether you do not know if the statements in the Complaint are true or not. Your answer also must be on 8 1/2 by 11 inch paper (the size of this page).

By filing an Answer in time, you keep your right to argue about this matter in court and to be notified of further proceedings.

Many people who have been served with lawsuits feel embarrassed or guilty about being in debt or being in an accident. Sometimes they just want it all to be over with, or they feel they should be punished and want the judge to punish them. **Even if you feel you are at fault, there is nothing wrong with filing an answer, and it does not mean that you are trying to avoid your legitimate debts.** You may disagree with the amount of money the plaintiff asked for in the Complaint. You may also want to answer to preserve your right to be notified of further hearings. If you do not file an Answer, you may lose your chance to say how much you think you should pay. However, you should know that filing an Answer may increase the court costs and attorney fees that you may owe if you lose the case.

You will need one original and two copies of your Answer. The original will be filed with the court, one copy will go to the plaintiff, and you will keep a copy. See the section below called "What to Do with the Answer" for the details on how this is done.

What is a Declaration of Exempt Income and Assets? It is a sworn statement that lets creditors know they can't garnish certain kinds of your income and assets.

There is no need to bring income and assets that are over the exemption limit to your creditor's attention. However, once your creditors find out about your assets and income that can be garnished or levied, they may do so anyway. Also, if you have income that exceeds the exempt amount, the excess can be garnished. Likewise, no matter what your property is worth, even if the creditor is not able to repossess it, they can still put a lien on it for the amount you owe.

How do I fill out the Answer?

The Caption. Look at your Summons and Complaint; you will notice that they have a heading that gives information about the case. This heading is called the "caption." All court papers, including the Summons, the Complaint, and your Answer, are called "pleadings." All pleadings use this same kind of caption. The caption may look something like this:

➢ In the _____Court of the State of _____In the County of _____

ABC Creditor

        Plaintiff   **Docket/File Number:**

John Doe

                    Civil Action

        Defendant   **SUMMONS**

➢ The top line gives the name of the court, the state, and the county. For instance: "District Court of Washington for Pierce County" or "In the Superior Court of the State of Washington In and for the County of Pierce."

➢ The left side lists the names of the Plaintiff and Defendant.

➢ The right side lists the **number** that has been assigned to this case by the court clerk (so that they can keep it filed correctly) and the **title** of that particular pleading.

Note: If the papers you received do not have a docket/file number, it may mean that the plaintiff decided to deliver (or serve) the papers to you before filing them with the court. In some states, the law allows this, and you are still bound by the time limit listed in your Summons. However, if this is the case, you may not need to file your Answer with the court yet. You will still have to deliver a copy to the plaintiff's lawyer (or the plaintiff if she/he has no lawyer). Read your Summons carefully. It should tell you what to do or you may need to contact the court directly.

Admission/Denials. After you complete the caption, use the middle of the page to give your answers to the statements in the Complaint. Usually, the paragraphs in the Complaint will be numbered. You may list the numbers and say one of three things about each paragraph of the Complaint:

You **admit** that it is a true statement (for instance, that you live in Monmouth County or that you are not a member of the Armed Forces). Admit the statement only if you agree with **every part** of it. Otherwise, deny the statement.

You **deny** that it is a true statement (for instance, that you owe a specific amount of money to the person named).

You write that you do not know whether the statement is true or not (for instance, the collection agency who is suing you is licensed and bonded. You might assume that they are, but you do not have any evidence; you have never seen their license).

Make sure you Read your Complaint carefully and make sure you briefly answer all the statements in it.

If you totally disagree with everything in the Complaint, you can simply write a single sentence saying you deny every allegation in the Complaint. However, you should not deny things that you know are true.

Defenses. You may also have technical or legal defenses to the Complaint, such as an argument that the statute of limitations has run. Actions to collect debts, like all actions, have a time limit called the "statute of limitations," which usually begins once the creditor has a right to sue you (for example, once you miss a payment). Once that time limit has passed, the person can no longer collect the money from you, and the action will be dismissed. For more information on the Statute of Limitations, check the Revised Code of Washington State Legislature (RCW)[2] at http://apps.leg.wa.gov/rcw/ or your local

---

[2] The Revised Code of Washington (RCW) is the compilation of all permanent laws now in force. It is a collection of Session Laws (enacted by the Legislature, and signed by the Governor, or enacted via the initiative process), arranged by topic, with amendments added and repealed laws removed. It does not include temporary laws such as appropriations acts. The official version of the RCW is published by the Statute Law Committee and the Code Reviser.

library should be able to help you find the right section of the RCW using the index. You may also argue as an affirmative defense that you do not owe the money. Even if you did buy the item for which the plaintiff is suing, you might not owe the money if the item was defective and you returned it or attempted to return it.

You could lose some "Affirmative Defenses" if you file an Answer without stating them. Affirmative Defenses are also listed in Rule 8(c) of the Civil Rules for Superior Court, available at your local law library.

Counterclaims. In some situations, you may have claims that you want to make against the plaintiff. These claims **must** be stated in your Answer if they arise out of the same transaction or occurrence that the plaintiff is suing about. For example, if you are being sued by the seller for a debt for purchase of an appliance that was defective and injured you, any claim you wish to make against the seller/plaintiff must be stated in your Answer. Or, if the plaintiff violated Fair Debt Collection rules, you may have a damage claim against the plaintiff. For more information on counterclaims, consult a lawyer or the court rules.

Exempt Income. If your income is exempt from garnishment, then you may wish to include a paragraph in your answer making the plaintiff aware of that fact. For example, if your only income is Social Security, which is exempt from garnishment by federal law, then you might write in your answer the following: "My income consists only of Social Security." While this is not a defense to the underlying lawsuit, it does provide the plaintiff with knowledge that your only income is exempt from garnishment. If you lose the lawsuit and the plaintiff subsequently garnishes your bank account containing exempt funds, then you may have a cause of action against the plaintiff.

The Signature and Your Address. On the last page, put the date you sign your name. Below that, sign your name with your legal signature (the one you use for checks). Just below your signature, print or type your name so it will be easily readable. Finally, put your address below that. Now your Answer is complete. You need to be able to receive delivery by mail and **by hand** at this address, so do not use a P.O. Box. It is important that you use an address where you know you will definitely receive your mail. Notices of hearings will be mailed to that address, and if you fail to appear because you didn't get the notice, a judgment may be entered against you by default.

Delivery. Make at least two copies of your Answer and Notice of Appearance. Deliver one copy of each of these documents to the lawyer for the plaintiff. The lawyer's name and address should be printed on the lower right-hand side of the Summons and Complaint. If the plaintiff doesn't have a lawyer and is representing himself, deliver a copy of the documents to the plaintiff. If you do not want to deliver them yourself, have a reliable friend do it for you. You must deliver a copy of your Answer or Notice of Appearance on or before the date stated in the Summons. Because it is important for your Answer and Notice of Appearance to be delivered on time, it is best to deliver a copy of each document personally to the plaintiff's lawyer. The papers may be left with a secretary or receptionist. If you are delivering the papers to the lawyer's office, ask the receptionist to stamp the original and copy of each document with a "copy received" stamp showing the date received.

Getting your original and copy of the Answer and Notice of Appearance stamped by the receptionist will prove that these documents were delivered by the deadline stated in the Summons. If you decide to mail these documents to the plaintiff's lawyer, be sure to allow enough time for the mail to be delivered by the deadline (at least three days). It is not enough for the Answer and Notice of Appearance to be postmarked on or before the deadline. It must be received by the deadline stated in the Summons. Also, if you mail the Answer, you should consider sending one Answer by regular mail and one by certified mail, return receipt requested. Hand-delivery is best because you can have the lawyer's office stamp the original and your copy that shows that your Answer was delivered on time.

If you mail the Notice of Appearance and/or the Answer, the court needs to know this was done. You do this by completing a Certificate of Service and attaching it to the original of the document that was mailed. A sample Certificate of Service and a Certificate of Service form you may use are attached. Be sure to make extra copies of the form before you use it. Make sure you identify what kind of legal paper the Certificate of Service refers to (i.e., Answer, Notice of Appearance, etc.) and strike out the type of delivery that does not apply (i.e., if you mailed it, strike out the words "hand-delivered").

Filing Your Answer. When the plaintiff pays the filing fee and files the Complaint with the court, the court assigns a case number. That number will usually be stamped or typed on the upper right-hand side of the Summons and Complaint. The court will not have any record of the case and will not be able to give you any information about the case until the case has been filed. If there is a case number on your Summons and Complaint, then you should write in the number on your Answer and Notice of Appearance and file the original(s) with the Court Clerk. File the original Answer and Notice of Appearance after you deliver a copy to the plaintiff's attorney and obtain proof of service (the "copy received" stamp), but before the deadline stated in the Summons. At the time you file the original Answer and Notice of Appearance you should stamp your personal copies with the Clerk's stamp showing the date the originals were filed.

If the Summons and Complaint that you received do not have a case number on them, then the Clerk will not have a record of your case and you will not be able to file the original of your Answer and Notice of Appearance. You must still follow the regular procedure for delivering a copy of your Answer to the plaintiff's lawyer, even if the case has not been filed. However, if there is no case number, keep your original Answer and Notice of Appearance until you are notified that the case has been filed and has been assigned a case number. When you receive the case number, follow the procedure for filing the original documents described above.

Remember to make sure that you file your Answer within the time limit listed in your Summons (usually 20 to 30 days). Do not take a chance with that time limit! Once you have timely filed your Answer and served the plaintiff's lawyer, you should be given notice of any hearings. Do not miss these hearings. If you have already missed your time limit, file an answer anyway. A late Answer may be better than no Answer at all. If you are too late, and a judgment has been entered against you, you should contact a lawyer immediately or file a Motion to Vacate.

JUDGMENTS

When a debt is in collections with an attorney and you are served with a lawsuit, you are generally given about 30 days to file an answer. If you can prove that the debt is invalid you can get the hearing dismissed. Additionally, if an agency has sued you without giving you the mandatory 30-day notice to dispute the validity of a debt (consumer right notice) then that is a violation of the Fair Debt Collection Practice Act (FDCPA). But if the debt is yours and you know it then you should contact the judgment creditor (JC) as soon as you are served. You want to avoid the entry of judgment at all costs because it will simply ruin your credit. Call, fax, or mail a request to the attorney suing you and offer a settlement in exchange for dismissing the case.

There may be several ways to remove a judgment from your credit reports. First, is the judgment still legally allowed to be on your credit reports? Look at the SOL for judgments and if your state allows it to be renewed. If it is still *legally* on your credit reports you should dispute it to the credit bureaus before you contact the JC. It may be deleted without ever paying it! This is because many court records are not verified in time when disputed. The bureau has 30 days to verify the accuracy of an item and to send a request to the courts and to expect a reply within 30 days is a long shot. We all know how slow the courts can be. If the court does not verify the judgment within 30 days, the credit bureau will delete it.

However, if the item has been verified as timely and you have no other documentation to prove it is not valid, then you can negotiate a settlement with the JC to dismiss the judgment. This is a much better rating than a "paid judgment." It tends to indicate that it was dismissed and is therefore "legally void." This is a better rating than showing you simply paid it—that means you owed it. Not much of a credit improvement. Make sure when you negotiate with the JC that you put your terms in writing and have the JC sign and date it. This can be used for proof later if the rating doesn't change. Once you agree, the JC will complete a form to dismiss the judgment and file it with the court. All public records are reported to credit bureaus so you should see your new rating in about 30 to 45 days.

Finally, there is a procedure called a "motion to vacate" a judgment. This procedure can be used if you have good cause to believe you were sued in error, were exempt because of retirement or SSI or were served improperly. The great news is that about 80% of judgments are awarded in error—you just have to know what to look for. Getting the judgment vacated means it does not stay on your credit and you do not have to pay it so if you think you have a good case for a vacate motion then by all means seriously consider pursuing it. Contact an attorney about this issue. You can attempt to vacate the judgment yourself but we recommend using an attorney.

Avoid judgments at all costs. The SOL on judgments is long—very long, usually 12 to 20 years and many are renewable (a judgment may be renewed if the creditor files a new suit seeking to renew the judgment prior to the expiration of the original judgment), therefore the judgment could follow you around forever. Even if you pay it you will be stuck with a "satisfied judgment" on your credit report for 7 years from date satisfied not filed! This can be a hopeless situation so avoid being sued at all costs. Be sure to always check your SOL for debts if you have been served because if it is expired (and many debts expire in four to 6 years) you can use that to dismiss the case. Many debtors are served every day for debts and they simply do not show up in court and a default judgment is entered against them—big mistake! Had half of them simply checked their SOL they would have found that the debt may have expired years before but since they did not dispute this, the judgment was awarded.

If you are sued, never let a judgment be entered. You have nothing to lose by disputing the validity of the judgment or even settling it out of court to avoid that nasty record landing on your credit reports. Even if you owe the debt and it is not legally expired under the SOL and you have no claim to vacate it, you should attempt to settle it out of court—before the court date so that it can be set aside. All the JC wants is their money so calling them to work out a settlement is the only smart thing to do. Otherwise, you may be forced to pay it later through wage levy or assets liens, not to mention the damage it will have done to your credit.

WAGE GARNISHMENT

Wage garnishment, the most common type of garnishment, is the process of deducting money from an employee's monetary compensation (including salary), sometimes as a result of a court order. In the United States, some such garnishments are limited by federal law to 25% of the disposable income that the employee earns. Wage garnishments continue until the entire debt is paid or arrangements are made to pay off the debt. Garnishments can be taken for any type of debt but common examples of debt that result in garnishments include:

> ➢ Child support

> ➢ Defaulted student loans

> ➢ State and federal taxes

> ➢ Unpaid court fines

> ➢ Any other type of monetary judgment

When served on an employer, garnishments are taken as part of the payroll process. When processing payroll, sometimes there is not enough money in the employee's net pay to satisfy all of the garnishments. In such a case, the correct order to take a garnishment must be satisfied. For example, in a case with federal tax, local tax, and credit card garnishments, the first garnishment taken would be the federal tax garnishments, then the local tax garnishments, and finally, garnishments for the credit card. Employers receive a notice telling them to withhold a certain amount of their employee's wages for payment and cannot refuse to garnish wages.

Wage garnishment can negatively affect credit, reputation, and the ability to receive a loan or open a bank account.

At present four U.S. states—North Carolina, Pennsylvania, South Carolina, and Texas—do not allow wage garnishment at all except for debts related to taxes, child support, federally guaranteed student loans, and court-ordered fines or restitution. Several other states observe maximum thresholds that are lower than the 25% maximum provided by federal law. States may also prohibit garnishment altogether in certain circumstances. For example, in

Florida the wages of a person who provides more than half the support for a child or other dependent are exempt from garnishment altogether (though this exemption is subject to waiver). Loans and negotiations with creditors can also help debtors to avoid wage garnishment.

In many states when the person is an employee or appointee of a governmental unit the writ is called a Writ of Sequestration. These are processed by the courts in the same manner as garnishments and are subject to the same wage exemptions.

The debtor has a remedy if he/she believes the Garnishment is improper under the law. That remedy is a Motion to Quash the Writ.

Debtors can have multiple writs of garnishment against their wages but most states follow the *first to serve rule*. The first to serve rule is that the employer must honor the garnishments one at a time in the order that they were served on the employer.

The other type of garnishment, also known as *attachment*, or attachment of earning, requires the garnishee to deliver all the defendant's money and/or property in the hands of the garnishee at the time of service of process to the court, to be paid over to the plaintiff. Since this type of garnishment is not continuing in nature, but is not subject to the type of restrictions that apply to wage garnishment, it is most often used against banks, or other persons or companies that incur liquidated obligations in the regular course of business. The garnishment should never begin during the pay period but should begin on the following pay period.

A wage garnishment is any legal or equitable procedure through which some portion of a person's earnings is required to be withheld by an employer for the payment of a debt. Most garnishments are made by court order. Other types of legal or equitable procedures include IRS or state tax collection agency levies for unpaid taxes and federal agency administrative garnishments for non-tax debts owed the federal government. Wage garnishments do not include voluntary wage assignments—that is, situations in which employees voluntarily agree that their employers may turn over some specified amount of their earnings to a creditor or creditors.

The Federal Wage Garnishment Law, Consumer Credit Protection Act Title 3 (CCPA) limits the amount of an employee's earnings that may be garnished and protects an employee from being fired if pay is garnished for only one debt. Title III is administered by the Wage and Hour Division of the Department of Labor's Employment Standards Administration. The Wage and Hour Division has no other authority with regard to garnishments. Questions over issues other than the amount being garnished or termination should be referred to the court or agency initiating the withholding action. For example, questions regarding the priority given to certain garnishments over others are not matters covered by Title III and may be referred to the court or agency initiating the garnishment action.

The law protects everyone receiving personal earnings, i.e., wages, salaries, commissions, bonuses, or other income—including earnings from a pension or retirement pension/program. Tips are generally not considered earnings for the purposes of the wage garnishment law. The law applies in all 50 states, the District of Columbia, and all U.S. territories and possessions.

What is the protection against discharge when wages are garnished? The CCPA prohibits an employer from firing an employee whose earnings are subject to garnishment for any one debt, regardless of the number of levies made or proceedings brought to collect that debt, because of the single garnishment. The Act does not prohibit discharge because an employee's earnings are separately garnished for two or more debts.

What are the restrictions on wage garnishment? The amount of pay subject to garnishment is based on an employee's "disposable earnings," which is the amount left after legally required deductions are made. Examples of such deductions include federal, state, and local taxes, the employee's share of State Unemployment Insurance and Social Security. It also includes withholdings for employee retirement systems required by law. Deductions not required by law—such as those for voluntary wage assignments, union dues, health and life insurance, contributions to charitable causes, purchases of savings bonds, retirement plan contributions (except those required by law), and payments to employers for payroll advances or purchases of merchandise—usually may not be subtracted from gross earnings when calculating disposable earnings under the CCPA.

The law sets the maximum amount that may be garnished in any workweek or pay period, regardless of the number of garnishment orders received by the employer. For ordinary garnishments (i.e., those not for support, bankruptcy, or any state or federal tax), the weekly amount may not exceed the lesser of two figures: 25% of the employee's disposable earnings, or the amount by which an employee's disposable earnings are greater than 30 times the federal minimum wage (currently $5.15 an hour). For example, if the pay period is weekly and disposable earnings are $154.50 ($5.15 X 30) or less, there can be no garnishment. If disposable earnings are more than $154.50 but less than $206.00 ($5.15 X 40), the amount above $154.50 can be garnished. A maximum of 25% can be garnished, if disposable income earnings are $206.00 or more. When pay periods cover more than one week, multiples of the weekly restrictions must be used to calculate the maximum amounts that may be garnished.

What about child support and alimony? Specific restrictions apply to court orders for child support or alimony. The garnishment law allows up to 50% of a worker's disposable earnings to be garnished for these purposes if the worker is supporting another spouse or child, or up to 60% if the worker is not. An additional 5% may be garnished for support payments more than 12 weeks in arrears.

Are there any exceptions to the law? The wage garnishment law specifies that the garnishment restrictions do not apply to certain bankruptcy court orders, or to debts due for federal or state taxes. If a state wage garnishment law differs from the CCPA, the law resulting in the smaller garnishment must be observed. You may be able to claim one or more exemptions and avoid paying the judgment or at least a portion of it.

Bank account funds that are from the following are exempt from garnishment:

➤ Veterans benefits

➤ Child support payments

➤ U.S. government pension

➤ Unemployment compensation

➤ Supplemental Security Income (SSI)

➤ Temporary Assistance for Needy Families

➤ Certain funds in a joint or community account

➤ Other public assistance or income allowed by state law

In order to protect your right to claim these exemptions you must, within specified days allowed from the date on the Writ of Garnishment, deliver to the court clerk and mail a copy to the plaintiff, the completed Exemption Claim Form.

U.S. FEDERAL TAX RULES GARNISHMENT

In the context of garnishments under U.S. federal tax law, there are only a few requirements that must be met before the Internal Revenue Service (IRS) starts a wage garnishment:

➤ The IRS must have assessed the tax and must have sent a written Notice and Demand for Payment.

➤ The taxpayer must have neglected or refused to pay the tax within the time prescribed in the notice; and.

➤ The IRS must have sent a Final Notice of Intent to Levy and Notice of Your Right to a hearing (levy notice) at least 30 days before the levy.

➤ A garnishment by the IRS is a form of administrative levy. In the case of an IRS levy, no court order is required.

The IRS may serve the Final Notice in person, may leave the notice at the taxpayer's home or usual place of business, or may send it to the last known address by certified or registered mail. The IRS is required to send the Final Notice to the last address known to the agency. The taxpayer does not need to actually receive the notice for the notice to be effective. Many taxpayers never actually receive the final notice. Those taxpayers may not realize they are in danger of receiving a levy until their wages are actually garnished.

LIENS

In other common-law countries, the term "lien" refers to a very specific type of security interest, being a passive right to retain (but not sell) property until the debt or other obligation is discharged. In contrast to the usage of the term in the United States, in other countries, it refers to a purely *possessory* form of security interest; indeed, when possession of the property is lost, the lien is released. However, common-law countries also recognize a slightly anomalous form of security interest called an "equitable lien," which arises in certain rare instances.

In the United States, liens can be consensual or nonconsensual (also termed voluntary or involuntary in different states). Consensual liens are imposed by a contract between the creditor and the debtor:

➤ Mortgage

➤ Auto lien

➤ Chattel mortgage

Nonconsensual liens typically arise by statute or by the operation of the common law, which gives a creditor the right to impose a lien on an item of real property or a chattel by the existence of the relationship of creditor and debtor. Those liens include the following:

➤ Tax liens, imposed to secure payment of a tax

➤ "Weed liens" and "demolition liens," assessed by the government to rectify a property from being a nuisance and public hazard

➤ Attorney's liens, against funds and documents to secure payment of fees

➤ Mechanic's liens, which secure payment for work done on property or land

➤ Judgment liens, imposed to secure payment of a judgment

➤ Maritime liens, imposed on ships by the admiralty

Liens are also "perfected" or "unperfected." Perfected liens are those liens for which a creditor has established a priority right in the encumbered property with respect to third-party creditors. Perfection is generally accomplished by taking the steps required by law to give third-party creditors notice of the lien. The fact that an item of property is in the hands of the creditor usually constitutes perfection. Where the property remains in the hands of the debtor, some further step must be taken, like recording a notice of the security interest with the appropriate office.

Perfecting a lien is an important part of the task of protecting the secured creditor's interest in the property. A perfected lien is valid against bona fide purchasers of property, and even against a trustee in bankruptcy; an unperfected lien may not be.

BAD CHECKS

Bad checks, also known as NSF (Not Sufficient Funds) checks, bounced checks, etc., can be a big problem for any credit department. There are both civil and criminal penalties for this unlawful act, although it is much more costly and difficult to prove a criminal case.

PAYMENTS FOR CASH ON DELIVERY VERSUS PREEXISTING DEBT

In most cases, NSF checks are not considered under the bad-check law if they are used to pay an antecedent debt. Therefore, if a debtor gives a creditor an

NSF check to pay a note payment or to pay an invoice that originally had open terms of credit, using an NSF check generally does not fall within the bad-check law of most states and jurisdictions. However, if the debtor provides a creditor with a NSF check for a COD order, then that act does fall within the bad-check laws.

POSTDATED CHECKS

Section 3-104(2)(b) of the UCC defines a check as "a draft drawn on a bank and payable on demand." A postdated check, since it is not payable on demand, does not satisfy this definition. Consequently, it has generally been held by most states that the giving of a postdated check does not constitute a present fraud nor is it within the scope of the bad-check laws.

While there are differences among the states as to how bad checks are viewed (whether a misdemeanor or a felony) and the remedies available to holders of the bad check against the drawer, there are several general factors that run through most state laws: In all states the maker of a check, who tenders a check knowing there is insufficient funds or credit behind the check, may be guilty of a crime and may be subject to civil penalties.

In the majority of states, the crime is treated as a misdemeanor. In states that make a distinction regarding a felony or misdemeanor, the amount of the check usually determines if the crime is a misdemeanor or a felony. In several states, the law provides for fines and or imprisonment, but does not specify if the crime is misdemeanor or felony. In some states, there is a criminal offense only when the bad check is given in exchange for property or for a present consideration. In other states, it is a criminal offense to issue a bad check with intent to defraud or with knowledge of insufficient funds. The intent to defraud and knowledge of insufficient funds is required to be present by most states' bad-check laws. The intent to defraud is sufficient. It is not necessary for the payee to have actually been defrauded.

In most states, statutory provisions provide that it is prima facie evidence of insufficient funds (or of intent to defraud) if (a) the check was not paid by the drawee (bank) on presentation for payment and (b) the drawer did not pay the check within a specified number of days after written notice to the drawer of dishonor of the check. The prescribed numbers of days for the various states are:

State	Days
Alabama	10 Days
Alaska	15 Days

Arizona	12 days
Arkansas	10 Days
California	30 Days
Colorado	15 Days
Connecticut	30 Days
Delaware	10 Days
District of Columbia	5 Days
Florida	7 Days
Georgia	10 Days
Hawaii	10 Days
Idaho	10 Days
Illinois	30 Days
Indiana	30 Days
Iowa	30 Days
Kansas	14 Days
Kentucky	10 Days
Louisiana	15 Days
Maine	10 Days
Maryland	10 Days
Massachusetts	2 Days
Michigan	30 Days
Minnesota	5 Days
Mississippi	15 days
Missouri	10 Days
Montana	5 Days
Nebraska	10 Days
Nevada	5 Days
New Hampshire	10 Days
New Jersey	35 Days
New Mexico	10 Days
New York	30 Days
North Carolina	30 Days
North Dakota	10 Days
Ohio	30 Days
Oklahoma	5 Days
Oregon	10 Days
Pennsylvania	10 Days
Rhode Island	7 Days

South Carolina	30 Days
South Dakota	30 Days
Tennessee	10 Days
Texas	10 Days
Utah	15 Days
Vermont	10 Days
Virginia	30 Days
Washington	15 Days
West Virginia	10 Days
Wisconsin	5 Days
Wyoming	5 Days

In many states the criminal provisions regarding bad checks do not apply to postdated checks. Because postdated checks are a promise to pay in the future, they are not technically viewed as checks. It has generally been held that postdated checks are not within the scope of most states' bad-check laws, and that the giving of a bad check in payment of a preexisting debt does not fall within the purview of most states' bad-check laws. Because the debt is preexisting, the maker of the check didn't deprive the payee of any right, procure anything of value from the payee, or wrongfully appropriate anything belonging to the payee.

On paper, the legal consequences for the maker of a bad check are usually quite severe; however, as a practical matter, the holder of a bad check may find it difficult to put into effect available remedies. In most localities, it is necessary to file a complaint with the appropriate criminal justice officer, such as a sheriff or district attorney, to initiate criminal legal action. In general, most of these criminal justice officers are too busy with other more serious crimes in the community. Therefore, the filing of a bad check criminal action will usually not be promptly acted upon, except in cases involving significant amounts of money. However, as a credit grantor you can effectively deal with the majority of routine bad check situations by putting into practice the following procedures:

Instruct your bank to redeposit any checks returned for insufficient or uncollected funds, which will effectively address any clerical errors the check's maker may have made regarding their bank account balance.

On checks still unpaid after redepositing or returned because payment was stopped, you should write to the maker advising them of the nonpayment, provide details of the check, and request in addition to the amount of the check, any appropriate service charges. It is suggested that the letter be sent certified mail with a return receipt requested. However, on small-balance bad checks the letter may be sent regular mail.

If the maker of a bad check does not respond to your notice and fails to make the check good, you should consider contacting an attorney in the locale/state where the bad-check writer is domiciled. They will be able to assist you with the collection of the bad check and put you in touch with legal counsel if you desire to discuss the legal remedies that may be available to you.

CHAPTER 12

START THE PROCESS OF REBUILDING YOUR CREDIT

REBUILDING CREDIT

Rebuilding your credit score is a simple process. There are specific steps you can take that will repair and improve your overall credit score. The negative records from the past cannot be erased. Negative records such as bankruptcy and collection accounts will remain on your credit report for 7 to 10 years, unless you negotiated otherwise with your creditors. But with a little work, you can improve your credit score. You can start the repair process before negative records expire. Below are five simple steps that you can take to repair and rebuild your credit.

Step 1: Research your debt. The first step to rebuilding your credit is to find out exactly where you stand. Order your credit report and score from all three credit reporting agencies (Experian, Equifax, TransUnion) by visiting www.freecredit.com, www.truecredit.com, or www.experian.com.

Print each report and examine it closely. Highlight all negative records or inaccuracies that are damaging your credit score. Make sure all the accounts listed are accurate.

Step 2: Check the expiration dates. Negative records will remain on your credit report for 7 to 10 years. The exact expiration date varies depending upon the type of record. Paying off an old collection debt or discharging your bankruptcy does not remove these records from your credit reports.

For each of the negative records on your credit report (including judgments, liens, charge-offs, late payments, bankruptcy filings, and collection records), look up the exact date they are set to expire from your credit report. You will likely see a major improvement in your credit score when these records expire.

Step 3: Dispute the errors. If you find inaccurate records, fraudulent accounts, or records that should have expired on your credit reports, you have the right to dispute these errors. You'll need to send a separate dispute letter to each of the credit bureaus to correct your Experian, Equifax, and TransUnion records. Once your dispute is received, the credit bureaus have 30 days to investigate and determine whether or not to make the change you have requested.

Do not try to dispute accurate or positive information that is listed on your credit report. Accurate information cannot be removed from your credit reports and it is a waste of time to attempt to dispute these records. Disputing positive information may actually harm your credit scores.

Step 4: Start adding positive information. Now that you know when your negative records will be removed from your credit report and you have disputed any inaccuracies, you are ready to start rebuilding your credit. Since there is no way to remove negative information from your credit report, the best way to improve your score is to add new positive information. Open up a new credit card secured or unsecured and use it responsibly each month. Keep your balances low and always pay your bills on time and in full each month.

Sign up for an online banking service that allows you to keep a close eye on your accounts. By not making any late payments, using credit responsibly, and avoiding unnecessary applications for credit, you are building a new history of good credit behavior on your credit report. Over time, you may want to open additional credit card accounts or obtain a loan to boost your credit score even higher.

Note: Aggressively applying for multiple credit cards can hurt your credit report as each inquiry is reported to the bureaus. Do not submit more than 6 applications yearly.

Step 5: Monitor your progress. It's easy to keep track of your credit score improvement with today's credit monitoring programs available. Instead of just giving you occasional access to your credit report and email alerts, these new credit monitoring programs include unlimited access to your credit reports and credit scores, identity theft insurance, credit score monitoring, daily alerts, and more. Once you have signed up for a credit monitoring service, you will be able to track your credit score progress closely. Your credit score should improve steadily as you continue to use credit responsibly and add new positive information to your credit reports.

CHAPTER 13

RESEARCHING YOUR DEBT

In researching your debt and credit rating it's often necessary to know the collection laws of a particular state. Because each state's laws will vary, knowing the correct collection law for your state and/or your creditor's state is essential.

Debts that are past the statute of limitations may be:

> ➤ Uncollectable

> ➤ Unreportable to the credit bureaus

> ➤ Capable of simple resolution

You do not have to deal with an abusive debt collector or old debts lingering on your credit report. You may be able to eliminate these problems under the Fair Debt Collection Practice Act (FDCPA) or the Fair Credit Reporting Act (FCRA). In some situations, you may even be able to sue the company violating your consumer rights.

Below are companies that are the top offenders in violating consumer rights. Keep in mind that there are more than 7,000 active collection agencies in the

United States alone, not including the "attorney" collector networks. Many collection agencies don't have the proper bonding and licensing requirements set forth in all states where they practice collections. Oftentimes, collections agencies inadvertently allow these requirements lapses and are not renewed. Others simply do not bother with obtaining the proper requirements.

1. First American Investment Company

2. Unifund CCR, Partners

3. Wolpoff & Abramson

4. Midland Credit Management

5. NCO Financial Systems

6. LVNV Funding (aka Resurgent Capital Services)

7. Costal Asset Management Group

8. Cach, LLC (has many attorney networks)

9. Frederick J. Hanna & Associates

10. Asset Acceptance

11. Collect America, LTD

12. Aurora Gold & Associates, LLC

These companies buy such a large volume of debt that they often only have a one-page affidavit of the debt. This is a big advantage to you in court, as the Plaintiff (creditor) has the burden of proof on them to prove the debt is owed. They most likely do not have:

1. The original contract/agreement

2. Past Statements of Account Activity

3. Proof of the date of last activity

With only an affidavit the creditor may not have enough supporting documentation to win in court. In many cases, they are relying on the statistical likelihood that you will not file an answer and let the lawsuit default to judgment.

WHAT IS A STATUTE OF LIMITATIONS (SOL)

The legal meaning for statute of limitations is: The time of commencing actions—that is, *time allowed that litigation lawsuit can be brought*. After that time, it has expired. A statute is a law passed by legislation. The original statute of limitations begins at the onset of the contract signing. Although the statute of limitations varies from state to state, it is usually 4 to 6 years, depending on the state. The term "statute of limitations" means the time allotted to legally enforce the debt. If a statute expires and someone sues you, it is up to you to bring an expired SOL defense to the other party's attention.

If you say nothing or do not bring up the expired statute then the judgment can be entered. Don't assume it means the other party is barred from attempting to collect. It simply means that your defense is the expired SOL not to enforce the lawsuit. If your statute of limitations has expired that means that the debt cannot be enforced by lawsuit; that does not dismiss the debt and the creditor can still leave it on your credit for 7 years (excluding some public records, those can remain for 10 years), but legally you do not have to pay it if the statute has expired.

Check your SOL appendix—it's a powerful tool for consumers. The SOL can thwart lawsuits and collectors. If a debt is legally expired, you can escape being sued or having to pay an old debt! Likewise, it can be detrimental because many debtors unwillingly renew the SOL by making a partial payment or a written promise to pay, which extends the statute.

The Statute of Limitations is a civil code. Each state has its own statute.

Many people confuse the statute of limitations to collect a debt with the time a debt is allowed to remain on your credit reports. The two are separate. Credit bureaus are allowed a certain time frame to report debts. Another big fear is that paying it will extend the time it is allowed to be reported on your credit. Debts are reported from *first* delinquency or written-off date, not by last activity or last payment. Exclusions would be tax liens; they remain from date paid for 7 to 10 years and can remain indefinitely if unpaid. Paying a debt will not restart the clock for reporting it, but you could restart the clock for collecting it; so, if you pay it, pay it in either full or restrictively. A promise to pay or partial payment can renew the statute in many states; many people think that only a renewed promise to pay does this. That's not the case—either can renew the statute.

SIGNED UNDER SEAL

"Signed under seal" can extend the SOL. A signed under seal provision is where some creditors will add it to the contract for further protection. It depends on the contract but generally, adding a signed under seal will enforce a longer SOL. The seal must be obvious, usually next to the terms on the front page. One also must consider state laws because some may enforce it while others do not. Read the Civil Procedure Code for your state and see if there is a mention of it. Not many creditors use a signed under seal, but some do. Courts have long recognized that the presence of the word "SEAL" next to and on the same line as the signature of an individual debtor on a promissory note is legally sufficient. Credit unions often use seals as added protection in case of default, bankruptcy, or an expired SOL.

In every state where there is the right to file suit on a debtor, there is also a time within which that suit may be filed. This is a powerful tool if you are aware of it. Just remember a partial payment, promise to pay, or regular payment on the debt can remove the limitation and the period can be renewed, but keep in mind that it depends on state law.

Some states don't allow the SOL to renew from a payment while others allow the "tolling of time" to start again, so look at your state rule and probably the state rule for where the debt was incurred. We know this can get tricky, but since the debt collector may be able to choose the state with longer SOL then possibly they too can choose the one with the extended SOL. Generally, the laws that govern the debt are the laws of the state that the debtor resides in.

FEDERAL TAXES

Tax liens remain on your credit reports for 7 to 10 years from the date satisfied, not filed. If they remain unpaid they can stay longer, however, they are only collectable for 7 to 10 years with some provisions. Keep in mind that the tolling of the time (SOL) can be extended by offer in compromise and payments

STATE TAXES

Federal taxes do expire, but many states have no SOL for state-owed taxes. To know for sure, you need to read your state's codes. Go to the Attorney General website at www.naag.org/attorneys general and click on your state. From there, locate your state laws and check. Usually it is under the Taxation and Finance Code. Or visit the State Taxation site, and remember if you read the code and cannot find an actual SOL for collecting the tax, then the absence of such usually means there is no SOL. You simply must read your own state law to see what the rule is for taxes. Some report from date paid, while others report from date opened or filed.

CHAPTER 14

STATUTE OF LIMITATION FOR DEBT, JUDGMENTS, AND TAXES, AND COLLECTION AGENCY LICENSE AND BONDING REQUIREMENTS FOR ALL STATES

In this chapter you will find bad-check laws, state collection requirements, statute of limitation for debts, judgments, and garnishments as well as license and bonding requirements for the collection agencies operating and/or collecting in your state. This information is invaluable and may be used in conjunction with a suit against the collection agency attempting to collect the debt.

The information provided below is on a state-by-state basis and includes information such as statute of limitations determinations. Please be advised statutes can change or be revised over time so be sure to check your state and the creditor's state for current laws.

What state should I use in figuring out the Statute of Limitations? The SOL can be either where the debtor resides or where the contract was signed. It has nothing to do with where the creditor is now.

What allows a creditor to use either state? Section 811 of the FDCPA. What about the SOL for Judgments? The statute for judgments is the state in which the judgment was entered. SOLs can be amended and change over time, so to be sure your SOL below is correct; check with your state Attorney Generals at www.naag.org/attorneys_general.

STATE: ALABAMA

INTEREST RATE

- Legal: 6%
- Judgment: 12%

STATUTE OF LIMITATIONS (IN YEARS)

- Open Account: 3
- Written Contract: 6
- Domestic Judgment: 20
- Foreign Judgment: 20

BAD-CHECK LAWS (CIVIL PENALTY)

Greater of $10 or Actual Bank Charges

GENERAL GARNISHMENT EXEMPTIONS

75% of wages are exempt from garnishment

COLLECTION AGENCY BOND & LICENSE

- Bond: No
- License: Yes
- Fee:

  - $25 - Population under 20,000
  - $100 - Population over 20,000

- Exemption for out-of-state collectors: Business license not required for out-of-state agency.

STATE: ALASKA

INTEREST RATE

- Legal: 10.5%
- Judgment: 10.5% or contractual

STATUTE OF LIMITATIONS (IN YEARS)

- Sale of Goods: 4
- Written Contract: 6
- Domestic Judgment: 10
- Foreign Judgment: 10

BAD-CHECK LAWS (CIVIL PENALTY)

The bidder may recover damages in an amount equal to $100 or treble the amount, whichever is greater, except that damages recovered under the bad-check law may not exceed the amount of the check by more than $1000.

GENERAL GARNISHMENT EXEMPTIONS

75% of employee's weekly net income or $402.50, whichever is more.

COLLECTION AGENCY BOND & LICENSE

- Bond: $5000 License: Yes
- Fee:

    - $100 - Application
    - $200 - Agency Biennially

STATE: ARIZONA

INTEREST RATE

- Legal: 10%
- Judgment: 10% or contractual

STATUTE OF LIMITATIONS (IN YEARS)

- Open Account: 3
- Written Contract: 6 in AZ, 4 outside AZ
- Domestic Judgment: 5, additional 5 upon request (indefinitely)
- Foreign Judgment: 4

BAD-CHECK LAWS (CIVIL PENALTY)

Twice the amount of the check or $50, whichever is greater, costs of suit, reasonable attorneys' fees.

GENERAL GARNISHMENT EXEMPTIONS

See federal law.

COLLECTION AGENCY BOND & LICENSE

- Bond: $10,000 minimum (based on gross income)
- License: Yes
- Fee:

  o $1,500 Application Fee
  o $600 Annual Fee
  o $23 per Officers/Managers

STATE: ARKANSAS

INTEREST RATE

- Legal: 6% or 5 points above the federal discount rate
- Judgment: Contract rate or 10% per annum, whichever is greater

STATUTE OF LIMITATIONS (IN YEARS)

- Open Account: 3
- Written Contract: 5 (partial payment stops the statute from running)
- Sale of Goods: (UCC-2) - 4
- Domestic Judgment: 10 - Renewable

- Foreign Judgment: 10

BAD-CHECK LAWS (CIVIL PENALTY)

Amount due, service charge not to exceed $10. On stop payment, 15 days following written demand to drawer's last-known address, holder may collect fee not to exceed $15; failure to make restitution and pay collection fee will result in liability of twice the amount of check but in no event less than $50.

GENERAL GARNISHMENT EXEMPTIONS

$500 head of family; $200 single. Includes personal property except clothing.

COLLECTION AGENCY BOND & LICENSE

- Bond: $5,000 to $25,000
- License: Yes
- Fee: $125 - $5 each employee

STATE: CALIFORNIA

INTEREST RATE

- Legal: 10%
- Judgment: 10% (Unless otherwise contracted)

STATUTE OF LIMITATIONS (IN YEARS)

- Open Account: Reduced to writing - 4
- Open Account: No writing - 2
- Written Contract: 4
- Domestic Judgment: 10 (renewable at 10)
- Foreign Judgment: 10 (commencing with judgment debtor's commencement of CA residence)

BAD-CHECK LAWS (CIVIL PENALTY)

Amount due, damages of treble the amount so owing, but in no case less than $100 or more than $500 per check.

GENERAL GARNISHMENT EXEMPTIONS

See federal law. Exemptions for necessities of life.

COLLECTION AGENCY BOND & LICENSE

No license or bond required.

STATE: COLORADO

INTEREST RATE

- Legal: 8%
- Judgment: 8% (or higher if specified in contract or note)

STATUTE OF LIMITATIONS (IN YEARS)

- Open Account: 3
- Written Contract: 6 (signed promissory note)
- Written Contract Goods Services: 3
- Domestic Judgment

  - District Court - 20 (renewable every 20)
  - County Court - 6 (renewable every 6)

- Foreign Judgment: 6 in CO

BAD-CHECK LAWS (CIVIL PENALTY)

Treble the amount of such check and in no case less than $100, including reasonable fees.

GENERAL GARNISHMENT EXEMPTIONS

See federal law.

COLLECTION AGENCY BOND & LICENSE

- Bond: $12,000 - $20,000
- License: Yes

- Fee: Determined by collection agency board
- Exemption for out-of-state collectors: Out of state collectors are exempt if (1) collecting only by interstate means (phone, fax, mail); (2) have no Colorado client; and (3) are regulated and licensed in the state in which they reside.

STATE: CONNECTICUT

INTEREST RATE

- Legal: 8%
- Judgment: 10%

STATUTE OF LIMITATIONS (IN YEARS)

- Open Account: 6
- Written Contract: 6
- Oral Contract: 3
- Domestic Judgment: 20/25
- Small Claims Judgment: 10/15
- Foreign Judgment: 20

BAD-CHECK LAWS (CIVIL PENALTY)

Amount of check plus lesser of: If no bank account, $750 or amount of check; or if insufficient funds, $400 or amount of check. Statutory form of notice must be sent at least two times. Statute does not apply to certain consumer services.

GENERAL GARNISHMENT EXEMPTIONS

25% of your disposable earnings may be garnished each week, or 40 times the federal minimum hourly wage, whichever is less.

COLLECTION AGENCY BOND & LICENSE

- Bond: $5000
- License: Yes

- Fee:

    o $200 Yearly
    o $50 Investigation

STATE: DELAWARE

INTEREST RATE

- Legal + Judgment
- Federal Reserve Discount Rate Plus 5% Points

STATUTE OF LIMITATIONS (IN YEARS)

- Sale of Goods: 4
- Open Account: 4
- Written Contract: 3
- Domestic Judgment: No provision
- Foreign Judgment: No provision

BAD-CHECK LAWS (CIVIL PENALTY)

Amount due, cost of suit, protest fees

GENERAL GARNISHMENT EXEMPTIONS

85% of disposable earnings or disposable earnings minus $150 weekly according to schedule.

COLLECTION AGENCY BOND & LICENSE

- Bond: No
- License: Merc. License
- Fee: $50 Yearly

DISTRICT OF COLUMBIA

INTEREST RATE

- Legal: 6%
- Judgment: 70% of interest rate on taxes to IRS

STATUTE OF LIMITATIONS (IN YEARS)

- Open Account: 3
- Written Contract: 3
- Domestic Judgment: 20
- Foreign Judgment: Foreign Statute

BAD-CHECK LAWS (CIVIL PENALTY)

Amount Due - Protest Fees

GENERAL GARNISHMENT EXEMPTIONS

See federal law. D.C. Government employees are not attachable.

COLLECTION AGENCY BOND & LICENSE

- Bond: No
- License: No
- Fee: No

STATE: FLORIDA

INTEREST RATE

- Legal: 10%
- Judgment: 10% or up to 18% if contractual

STATUTE OF LIMITATIONS (IN YEARS)

- Open Account: 4

- Written Contract: 5
- Domestic Judgment: 7 Renewable
- Foreign Judgment: 5 if not recorded instate

BAD-CHECK LAWS (CIVIL PENALTY)

In event of failure to make payment within 30 days after demand, treble amount owed in addition to the amount owed together with bank and court costs and reasonable attorneys' fees, not less than $50 and no more than $2,500. If payment is made in 30 days, a service charge of $10 or 5% of face amount of check, whichever is greater, can be added. In stop payment action, reimbursement for actual travel expenses to holder or agent for filing papers, and for traveling and providing witnesses to and from proceeding.

GENERAL GARNISHMENT EXEMPTIONS

- See federal law except 100% head of household.
- Liberal Homestead Exemption - first $1,000 of automobile

COLLECTION AGENCY BOND & LICENSE

- Bond: Yes - $50,000 (Commercial)
- License: Yes
- Fee: Yes

    - $200 - Registration
    - $50 - Investigation
    - $200 - Renewal

- Exemption for out-of-state collectors: Registration is required for out-of-state collectors if (1) soliciting accounts; (2) if client (creditor, its affiliate or subsidiary) has an office in Florida.

STATE: GEORGIA

INTEREST RATE

- Legal: 7%
- Judgment: 12%

- Commercial Accounts: 18%

STATUTE OF LIMITATIONS (IN YEARS)

- Open Account: 4
- Written Contract: 6
- Domestic Judgment: 7
- Foreign Judgment: 5

BAD-CHECK LAWS (CIVIL PENALTY)

Upon 30 days following certified written demand by payee to maker, the maker shall be liable to the payee for damages of double the amount owing on the check not to exceed $500 and service charge not to exceed $15.

GENERAL GARNISHMENT EXEMPTIONS

See federal law. City, County & State employees may be garnished.

COLLECTION AGENCY BOND & LICENSE

- Bond: No
- License: No
- Fee: No

STATE: HAWAII

INTEREST RATE

- Legal: 10% (no written contract)
- Judgment: 10% (no written contract)

STATUTE OF LIMITATIONS (IN YEARS)

- Sale of Goods: 6
- Open Account: 6
- Written Contract: 6
- Domestic Judgment: 10
- Foreign Judgment: 6 for Regis./10 after Regis.

BAD-CHECK LAWS (CIVIL PENALTY)

Damages equal to $100 or triple amount of check, not to exceed $500.

GENERAL GARNISHMENT EXEMPTIONS

95% of first $100, 90% of second $100, 80% of net wages in excess of $200 per month or federal limits whichever is greater.

COLLECTION AGENCY BOND & LICENSE

- Bond: $25,000/$15,000 each branch
- License: Registration with "DCCA" required for consumer, not commercial, collections
- Fee:

  - $ 25 - Application
  - $ 80 - Registration
  - $ 50 - Compliance
  - $155 for 2 years

STATE: IDAHO

INTEREST RATE

- Legal: 12%
- Judgment: 10.875% plus the base rate

STATUTE OF LIMITATIONS (IN YEARS)

- Open Account: 4
- Oral Contract: 4
- Written Contract: 5
- Domestic Judgment: 5 renewable
- Foreign Judgment: 6 renewable

BAD-CHECK LAWS (CIVIL PENALTY)

$100 or treble the amount of the check, whichever is greater, but not more than $500 greater than the amount of the check.

GENERAL GARNISHMENT EXEMPTIONS

See federal law.

COLLECTION AGENCY BOND & LICENSE

- Bond: $5,000 initial
- License: Yes
- Fee: $100 - permit fee $50 - renewal
- Exemption for out-of-state collectors: Out-of-state collectors may qualify for a special license if (1) only collecting for client; and (2) are licensed and bonded by any state.

STATE: ILLINOIS

INTEREST RATE

- Legal: 5%
- Judgment: 9%

STATUTE OF LIMITATIONS (IN YEARS)

- Sales (UCC): 4
- Open Account: 5
- Written Contract: 10
- Domestic Judgment: 20
- Foreign Judgment: Same as foreign jurisdiction

BAD-CHECK LAWS (CIVIL PENALTY)

Treble amount of check but not less than $100 nor more than $500 plus attorney's fees and court costs.

GENERAL GARNISHMENT EXEMPTIONS

15% of gross wages or disposable earnings for workweek up to 45 times the federal minimum hourly wage, whichever is greater.

COLLECTION AGENCY BOND & LICENSE

- Bond: $25,000
- License: Yes
- Fee:

    o $750 - Original
    o $750 - Renewal

- Exemption for out-of-state collectors: Out-of-state collectors may be exempt if (1) not soliciting accounts in Illinois; (2) their state of residence has laws which provide similar reciprocity (allow out-of-state agencies to collect only); and (3) the state in which the non-Illinois agency resides extends the same privileges to out-of-state agencies.

STATE: INDIANA

INTEREST RATE

- Legal: 8%
- Judgment: 8%

STATUTE OF LIMITATIONS (IN YEARS)

- Open Account: 6
- Written Contract for payment of money

    o (executed before 9/1/82): 10
    o (executed after 8/31/82): 6

- Written Contract (other than payment of money): 10
- Written Contract for sale of goods: 4
- Domestic Judgment:

    o 10 on real estate
    o 20 against the person

- Foreign Judgment: 10

BAD-CHECK LAWS (CIVIL PENALTY)

Treble amount of check not to exceed $500 plus amount of check, attorney's fees of not less than $100 and interest at 18% per annum.

GENERAL WAGE GARNISHMENT EXEMPTIONS

75% of disposable earnings for work week or the amount of 30 times the federal minimum hourly wage, whichever is greater.

COLLECTION AGENCY BOND & LICENSE

- Bond: $5000 each office
- License: Yes
- Fee:

  o $100 plus $5 per annum, each unlicensed employee
  o $30 branch office
  o $80 - Renewal

- Exemption for out-of-state collectors: Out-of-state collectors are exempt from licensing if (1) collecting for a nonresident creditor; and (2) collection activities limited to interstate communications (phone, fax, mail).

STATE: IOWA

INTEREST RATE

- Legal: 5%
- Judgment: 10%

STATUTE OF LIMITATIONS (IN YEARS)

- Open Account: 5
- Written Contract: 10
- Domestic Judgment: 10 - can be renewed in the 9th year

- Foreign Judgment: 10 - can be renewed in the 9th year

BAD-CHECK LAWS (CIVIL PENALTY)

Treble amount of dishonored check but not to exceed amount of check plus $500.

GENERAL GARNISHMENT EXEMPTIONS

See federal law.

COLLECTION AGENCY BOND & LICENSE

- Bond: No
- License: No
- Fee: No

STATE: KANSAS

INTEREST RATE

- Legal: 10%
- Judgment: 12%

STATUTE OF LIMITATIONS (IN YEARS)

- Open Account: 3
- Written Contract: 5
- Domestic Judgment: 5 renewable
- Foreign Judgment: 5 renewable

BAD-CHECK LAWS (CIVIL PENALTY) Giver of worthless check is liable for the amount of the check plus an amount equal to the greater of the following: (a) treble the amount of the check, but not exceeding the amount of the check by more than $500; or (b) $100.

GENERAL GARNISHMENT EXEMPTIONS

- See federal law
- Plus other personal property, benefit exemptions, and homestead

COLLECTION AGENCY BOND & LICENSE

- Bond: No
- License: No
- Fee: No

STATE: KENTUCKY

INTEREST RATE

- Legal: 8%
- Judgment: 12%

STATUTE OF LIMITATIONS (IN YEARS)

- Open Account: 5
- Written Contract: 15
- Oral Contract: 5
- Domestic Judgment: 15
- Foreign Judgment: 15

BAD-CHECK LAWS (CIVIL PENALTY)

N/A

GENERAL GARNISHMENT EXEMPTIONS

75% of disposable income or 30 times the federal minimum hourly wage (whichever is greater)

COLLECTION AGENCY BOND & LICENSE

- Bond: No
- License: No
- Fee: No

STATE: LOUISIANA

INTEREST RATE

- Legal: 9.75%
- Judgment: 9.75%

STATUTE OF LIMITATIONS (IN YEARS)

- Open Account: 3
- Written Contract: 10
- Promissory Notes: 5
- Domestic Judgment: 10
- Foreign Judgment: 10

BAD-CHECK LAWS (CIVIL PENALTY)

Drawer of dishonored check who fails to pay 30 days after written demand delivered by certified or registered mail is liable for damages equal to twice amount owing but not less than $100 plus attorney's fees and court costs. Payee may charge service charge not to exceed $15 or 5% of the face amount of the check, whichever is greater.

District Attorney can collect fees for issuance of worthless check, depending on the amount of the check.

GENERAL GARNISHMENT EXEMPTIONS

75% disposable earnings per work week, but not less than 30 times the federal minimum hourly wage.

COLLECTION AGENCY BOND & LICENSE

- Bond: Yes - $10,000
- License: Yes
- Fee:

  o $200 Initial
  o $200 Investigation
  o $200 Renewal

- o $100 Branch
- o $100 Branch Renewal

STATE: MAINE

INTEREST RATE

- Legal: 8%
- Post Judgment: 15% annual (less than $30,000) T-Bill rate over $30,000

STATUTE OF LIMITATIONS (IN YEARS)

- Open Account: 6
- Written Contract: 6 + 20 (with attestment)
- Domestic Judgment: 20
- Foreign Judgment: 20

BAD-CHECK LAWS (CIVIL PENALTY)

Amount due, court costs, service costs, collection costs, processing charges can be recovered only if statutory notice given, or payment within 10 days of notice.

GENERAL GARNISHMENT EXEMPTIONS

You may garnish 25% of disposable income or 40 times the federal minimum wages per week (whichever is less). After judgment only.

COLLECTION AGENCY BOND & LICENSE

- Bond: $25,000 to $50,000
- License: Yes
- Fee: $400 Yearly
- Exemption for out-of-state collectors: Contact state authority. Licensing authority is allowing some exemptions to out-of-state agencies that collect for nonresident creditors and are not soliciting.

STATE: MARYLAND

INTEREST RATE

- Legal: 6%
- Judgment: 10% or contractual

STATUTE OF LIMITATIONS (IN YEARS)

- Open Account: 3
- UCC: 4
- Specialty: 12 (contract under seal)
- Written Contract: 3
- Domestic Judgment: 12
- Foreign Judgment: 12

BAD-CHECK LAWS (CIVIL PENALTY)

Amount due, $15 fee, and amount up to two times the amount of the check, but not more than $1,000. Holder may claim damages 30 days after mailing notice of dishonor to last known address of maker or drawer.

GENERAL GARNISHMENT EXEMPTIONS

Greater of 75% or amount = to $145 x no. of wks. in which wages due were earned; except in Caroline, Worchester, Kent, & Queen Anne's Counties, see federal law. Exemption is up to $3,000 in cash and/or property for non-wage property exemption.

COLLECTION AGENCY BOND & LICENSE

- Bond: $5000
- License: Yes
- Fee: $200 each office

STATE: MASSACHUSETTS

INTEREST RATE

- Legal: 6%
- Judgment: 12%
- Contract: 12%

STATUTE OF LIMITATIONS (IN YEARS)

- Open Account on Contract: 6
- Contract: 6
- Sales (UCC) Contract: 4
- Domestic Judgment: 20 (presumed satisfied after 20 years)
- Foreign Judgment: 20
- Contracts Under Seal: 20

BAD-CHECK LAWS (CIVIL PENALTY)

- Amount due, costs of suit, protest fees
- Additional damages $100 - $500 can be assessed.

GENERAL GARNISHMENT EXEMPTIONS

$125 week

COLLECTION AGENCY BOND & LICENSE

- Bond: $10,000 - $25,000
- License: Yes
- Fee: Determined by commissioner

STATE: MICHIGAN

INTEREST RATE

- Legal: 5%
- Judgment: 7.162 changes semiannually
- Usury limit: 25%

STATUTE OF LIMITATIONS (IN YEARS)

- Open Account: 6
- Written Contract: 6
- Sales (UCC) Contract: 4
- Domestic Judgment: 10 renewable
- Foreign Judgment: 10

BAD-CHECK LAWS (CIVIL PENALTY)

- Twice the amount of check - not to exceed $500.
- Retail Claims - Notice Requirements.

GENERAL GARNISHMENT EXEMPTIONS

See federal law.

COLLECTION AGENCY BOND & LICENSE (RETAIL ONLY)

- Bond: $5,000 - $50,000
- License: Yes
- Fee:

  - $150 - Investigation
  - $225 - Initial
  - $125 - Annually

- Exemption for out-of-state collectors: Out-of-state collectors are exempt if (1) collecting by interstate means; and (2) have no clients in the state of Michigan.

STATE: MINNESOTA

INTEREST RATE

- Legal: 6%
- Judgment: 5% (Changes yearly)
- Business or Agricultural Loan: 4.5% over federal discount rate

STATUTE OF LIMITATIONS (IN YEARS)

- Goods Sold & Delivered (UCC): 4
- Open Account: 6
- Written Contract: 6
- Transportation Service: 3
- Domestic Judgment: 10
- Foreign Judgment: 10

BAD-CHECK LAWS (CIVIL PENALTY)

$100 or up to 100% of the value of the check, whichever is greater, plus interest at the rate payable on judgments on the face amount of check, plus reasonable attorney fees if aggregate amount of checks within 6-month period is over $1250.

GENERAL GARNISHMENT EXEMPTIONS

Greater of 75% or amount equal to 40 times the federal minimum hourly wage.

COLLECTION AGENCY BOND & LICENSE

- Bond: $5,000 to $20,000
- License: Yes
- Fee:

  o $1,000 - Initial
  o $400 - Annual
  o $10 - Per Collector

STATE: MISSISSIPPI

INTEREST RATE

- Legal: 8%
- Judgment: Amount in contract if no contract amount court decides

STATUTE OF LIMITATIONS (IN YEARS)

- Open Account: 3
- Written Contract: 3
- UCC: 6
- Domestic Judgment: 7
- Foreign Judgment: 7 (3 if resident)

BAD-CHECK LAWS (CIVIL PENALTY)

On checks up to and including $25.00, additional damages would be 100% of check amount. On checks from $25.01 to $200.00, additional damages would be 50% of check amount but not less than $25.00. On checks over $200.00 additional damages would be 25% of check amount.

GENERAL GARNISHMENT EXEMPTIONS

See federal law.

COLLECTION AGENCY BOND & LICENSE

- Bond: No
- License: City-Business
- Fee: $15-$50

STATE: MISSOURI

INTEREST RATE

- Legal: 9%
- Judgment: 9%

STATUTE OF LIMITATIONS (IN YEARS)

- Sale of Goods: 4
- Open Account: 5
- Written Contract: 10
- Money & Property:

  o   Domestic Judgment: 10 (Revived every 3 years)
  o   Foreign Judgment: 10 (Revived every 3 years)

BAD-CHECK LAWS (CIVIL PENALTY)

Greater of treble face amount owed or $100. Damages should not exceed $500 (Exclusive of attorney fees).

GENERAL GARNISHMENT EXEMPTIONS

See federal law; exempt 90% of week's net pay, head of household, single person w/o depend. = 75%

COLLECTION AGENCY BOND & LICENSE

- Bond: No
- License: No
- Fee: No

STATE: MONTANA

INTEREST RATE

- Legal: 10%
- Judgment: 10%
- A binding written agreement may provide for interest of 15% or 6% above prime

STATUTE OF LIMITATIONS (IN YEARS)

- Open Account: 5

- Written Contract: 8
- Domestic Judgment: 6 (over $5,000) Renewable
- Foreign Judgment: 6 Renewable

BAD-CHECK LAWS (CIVIL PENALTY)

$100 or treble amount of check, but in no case may damages exceed $500.

GENERAL GARNISHMENT EXEMPTIONS

See federal law.

COLLECTION AGENCY BOND & LICENSE

- Bond: No
- License: No
- Fee: No

Caveats: Foreign corporations should register with MT Sec. of State prior to any suit in MT Courts or risk dismissal.

Attorney fees only if provided by a signed written <u>agreement</u>.

STATE: NEBRASKA

INTEREST RATE

- Legal: 12% per written instrument or contract rate
- Judgment: 1% above bond equivalent yield as published by U.S. Treasury

STATUTE OF LIMITATIONS (IN YEARS)

- Open Account: 4
- Written Contract: 5
- Domestic Judgment: 5, renewable every 5
- Foreign Judgment: 5 nonrenewable

BAD-CHECK LAWS (CIVIL PENALTY)

Amount due, costs, protest fees

GENERAL GARNISHMENT EXEMPTIONS

Greater of 75% disposable earnings (85% if head of household), or 30 times the federal minimum hourly wage.

COLLECTION AGENCY BOND & LICENSE

- Bond: Based on Lic. Solic. Less Than 5 = 5,000, 5-15 = $10,000, 16-Up = $15,000
- License: Yes
- Fee: (not to exceed)

  - $250 - Investigation
  - $200 - Original
  - $100 - Renewal
  - $50 - Investigation Branch Office
  - $35 - Original Branch Office

- Exemption for out-of-state collectors: Out-of-state collectors are exempt if (1) communicating by interstate means (phone, fax, mail); and (2) are "regulated" by the laws of another state.

STATE: NEVADA

INTEREST RATE

- Legal: 2% Over Prime
- Judgment: 2% Over Prime

STATUTE OF LIMITATIONS (IN YEARS)

- Open Account: 4
- Written Contract: 6
- Lease: 4
- Domestic Judgment: 6

- Foreign Judgment: 6

BAD-CHECK LAWS (CIVIL PENALTY)

Amount due, protest fees three times check amount not more than $500, or less than $100

GENERAL GARNISHMENT EXEMPTIONS

Garnish only. 25% of disposable earnings for each week or 30 times federal minimum hourly wage (whichever is less)

COLLECTION AGENCY BOND & LICENSE

- Bond: $25,000 to $50,000
- License: Yes
- Fee:
  - $250 - App. Survey
  - $300 - Original
  - $200 - Renewal
- Exemption for out-of-state collectors: Out-of-state collectors are exempt if (1) collecting by interstate means (phone, fax, mail); and (2) collecting for an out-of-state client.

STATE: NEW HAMPSHIRE

INTEREST RATE

- Judgment: 7.6%

STATUTE OF LIMITATIONS (IN YEARS)

- Open Account: 3
- For Goods: 4
- Written Contract: 3
- For Goods: 4
- Domestic Judgment: 20
- Foreign Judgment: 20

BAD-CHECK LAWS (CIVIL PENALTY)

Amount due, interest, court costs, reasonable costs of collection, and $10 per day (maximum is $50). If check issued to city or town, amount due, $15 fee plus protest, bank, and legal fees; if issued to state agency, amount due, $5 fee plus protest and bank fees.

GENERAL GARNISHMENT EXEMPTIONS

50 times the federal minimum hourly wage—all future wages are exempt so that the court cannot issue an ongoing order.

COLLECTION AGENCY BOND & LICENSE

- Bond: No
- License: No
- Fee: No

STATE: NEW JERSEY

INTEREST RATE

- Legal: 6%
- Judgment: No Statutory Provision

STATUTE OF LIMITATIONS (IN YEARS)

- Open Account: 6
- Sale of Goods: 4
- Written Contract: 6
- Domestic Judgment: 20
- Foreign Judgment: 20

BAD-CHECK LAWS (CIVIL PENALTY)

N/A

GENERAL GARNISHMENT EXEMPTIONS

$142.50 week min. 10% of gross earnings $142.50 and over.

COLLECTION AGENCY BOND & LICENSE

- Bond: $5,000 Surety
- License: No
- Fee: No

STATE: NEW MEXICO

INTEREST RATE

- Judgment: 8.75% (in the absence of a written contract)

STATUTE OF LIMITATIONS (IN YEARS)

- Open Account: 4
- Written Contract: 6
- Domestic Judgment: 14
- Foreign Judgment: 14

BAD-CHECK LAWS (CIVIL PENALTY)

- Amount due, triple damages up to $500 per check.
- Complex requirements need to be met.

GENERAL GARNISHMENT EXEMPTIONS

Greater of 75% or amount each week equal to 40 times the federal minimum hourly wage.

COLLECTION AGENCY BOND & LICENSE

- Bond: $5,000 minimum, based on volume
- License: Yes
- Fee:

- o $500 - original collection agency or branch
- o $300 - renewal collection agency or branch
- o $100 - examination fee for manager's license
- o $50 - manager renewal

- Exemption for out-of-state collectors: Out-of-state agency is exempt if (1) collecting by interstate means (phone, fax, mail); and (2) debt was incurred outside the state of New Mexico.

STATE: NEW YORK

INTEREST RATE

- Legal: 16%
- Judgment: 9%

STATUTE OF LIMITATIONS (IN YEARS)

- Open Account: 6
- Written Contract: 6
- Domestic Judgment: 20 (10 yr. renewable lien)
- Foreign Judgment: 20 (10 yr. renewable lien)

BAD-CHECK LAWS (CIVIL PENALTY)

Face value of check plus two times check amount up to a maximum of $400 on NSF or $750 on "no account" (demand prescribed by law). GEN.OB.1.1-104

GENERAL GARNISHMENT EXEMPTIONS

90% of earnings, except first $127.50 week wholly exempt.

COLLECTION AGENCY BOND & LICENSE

- Bond: No
- License: No
- Fee: No
- Buffalo: $5,000 Bond - $50 fee

- NYC: License, $150 - 2 yr. fee

STATE: **NORTH CAROLINA**

INTEREST RATE

- Legal: 8%
- Judgment: 8%

STATUTE OF LIMITATIONS (IN YEARS)

- Open Account: 3
- Sale of Goods: 4
- Written Contract: 3
- Domestic Judgment: 10
- Foreign Judgment: 10

BAD-CHECK LAWS (CIVIL PENALTY)

30 day written demand lesser of $500 or treble amount owing on the check, but not less than $100.

GENERAL GARNISHMENT EXEMPTIONS

100% of last 60 days' earnings for family support. Garnishment only by political subdivisions for taxes, ambulance fees, etc.

COLLECTION AGENCY BOND & LICENSE

- Bond: $5,000 to $50,000
- License: Yes
- Fee: $500
- Exemption for out-of-state collectors: Contact state authorities. Unofficially, licensing authorities may allow out-of-state agencies to bypass requirements if they do not solicit in state and/or work for in-state clients.

STATE: NORTH DAKOTA

INTEREST RATE

- Legal: 6%
- Judgment: 12%

STATUTE OF LIMITATIONS (IN YEARS)

- Open Account for services: 6
- Sale of Goods: 4
- Written Contract: 6
- Domestic Judgment: 10 renewable
- Foreign Judgment: 10 renewable

BAD-CHECK LAWS (CIVIL PENALTY)

Amount due, collection fees of $20, and $100 or treble amount of check whichever is less.

GENERAL GARNISHMENT EXEMPTIONS

Greater of 75% or amount each week equal to 40 times the federal minimum hourly wage. Plus $20.00 each household dependent.

COLLECTION AGENCY BOND & LICENSE

- Bond: $20,000
- License: Yes
- Fee: $200
- Exemption for out-of-state collectors: Out-of-state collectors may be exempt if (1) collecting only; (2) their office is located in a state that has a reciprocal law; and (3) the state has "enacted similar legislation."

STATE: OHIO

INTEREST RATE

- Legal: 10%
- Judgment: 10%

STATUTE OF LIMITATIONS (IN YEARS)

- Open Account: 4
- Sales Contract (UCC2-725)
- Written Contract: 15
- Domestic Judgment: 21 renew every 5
- Foreign Judgment: 21 renew every 5

BAD-CHECK LAWS (CIVIL PENALTY)

The greater of $200 or three times the amount of check and attorney fees (no maximum).

GENERAL GARNISHMENT EXEMPTIONS

See federal law. Garnishment limited to once a month per employee.

COLLECTION AGENCY BOND & LICENSE

- Bond: No
- License: No
- Fee: No

STATE: OKLAHOMA

INTEREST RATE

- Legal: 6%
- Judgment: 4% over U.S. Treasury Bill Rate of previous year. (1996 = 9.55% 1997 = 9.15%)

STATUTE OF LIMITATIONS (IN YEARS)

- Open Account: 3
- Written Contract: 5
- Domestic Judgment: 5 renewable
- Foreign Judgment: 3

BAD-CHECK LAWS (CIVIL PENALTY)

N/A

GENERAL GARNISHMENT EXEMPTIONS

State law: 75% of earnings exempted, more if hardship established. All federal exemptions apply.

COLLECTION AGENCY BOND & LICENSE

- Bond: No
- License: No
- Fee: No

STATE: OREGON

INTEREST RATE

- Statutory + Judgment: 9% simple interest per annum (unless specified by contract)

STATUTE OF LIMITATIONS (IN YEARS)

- Open Account: 6
- Sale of Goods: 6 (4 years UCC Transaction)
- Written Contract: 6
- Domestic Judgment: 10 - renewable at 10
- Foreign Judgment: 10

BAD-CHECK LAWS (CIVIL PENALTY)

When maker fails to tender amount due after written demand made by payee, payee may recover damages in an amount equal to $100 or treble amount of the amount for which the check, draft, or order is drawn, whichever is greater, provided the amount is not greater than $500 over the due amount, if demand letter is sent to debtor 30 days before suit is filed.

GENERAL GARNISHMENT EXEMPTIONS

75% of disposable earnings or 40 times the federal minimum hourly wage.

COLLECTION AGENCY BOND & LICENSE

- Bond: No
- License: Registration only
- Fee: Established by director
- Exemption for out-of-state collectors: Contact state authorities. Out-of-state agencies may be exempt if (1) collecting for out-of-state client; (2) the debt was incurred by an Oregonian outside the state; and (3) the state where the collection agency is headquartered has a registration program comparable to Oregon's law.

STATE: PENNSYLVANIA

INTEREST RATE

- Legal: 6%
- Judgment: 6%

STATUTE OF LIMITATIONS (IN YEARS)

- Open Account: 4
- Written Contract: 4
- Domestic Judgment: 5 (writ of revival within 5 yrs.)
- Foreign Judgment: 4

    o Lien against real estate: 5 yrs.
    o Personal property Ex: 20 yrs.

BAD-CHECK LAWS (CIVIL PENALTY)

Upon written demand from payee following conviction for passing a bad check and failure to make restitution, the payee upon obtaining civil judgment is entitled to an amount equal to $100 or treble the amount for which the check is drawn, whichever is greater, not to exceed by more than $500 the value of the check.

GENERAL GARNISHMENT EXEMPTIONS

100% of wages, certain pensions, retirement accounts and Keogh plan under certain circumstances, and $300.

COLLECTION AGENCY BOND & LICENSE

- Bond: No
- License: No
- Fee: No

STATE: RHODE ISLAND

INTEREST RATE

- Legal: 12%
- Judgment: 12%

STATUTE OF LIMITATIONS (IN YEARS)

- Open Account: 10
- Written Contract: 10
- Domestic Judgment: 20
- Foreign Judgment: 20

BAD-CHECK LAWS (CIVIL PENALTY)

Amount of check plus fee of $25, plus amount up to treble amount of check but not less than $200 or more than $1,000.

GENERAL GARNISHMENT EXEMPTIONS

See federal law.

COLLECTION AGENCY BOND & LICENSE

- Bond: No
- License: No
- Fee: No

STATE: SOUTH CAROLINA

INTEREST RATE

- Legal: 8.75%
- Judgment: 12%

STATUTE OF LIMITATIONS (IN YEARS)

- Open Account: 3
- Written Contract: 3
- Domestic Judgment: 10
- Foreign Judgment: 10

BAD-CHECK LAWS (CIVIL PENALTY)

In addition to other fines, issuer shall pay all reasonable court costs, not to exceed $20, and if payment is not made within 30 days, issuer shall pay amount of check and damages, of the lesser of $500 or treble the amount of the check.

GENERAL GARNISHMENT EXEMPTIONS

100%

COLLECTION AGENCY BOND & LICENSE

- Bond: No

- License: Yes - all business
- Fee: No
- Exemption for out-of-state collectors: License required for in-state agency only.

STATE: SOUTH DAKOTA

INTEREST RATE

- Legal: 12%
- Judgment: 10%

STATUTE OF LIMITATIONS (IN YEARS)

- Open Account: 6
- Sale of Goods: 4
- Written Contract: 6
- Domestic Judgment: 20
- Foreign Judgment: 10

BAD-CHECK LAWS (CIVIL PENALTY)

N/A

GENERAL GARNISHMENT EXEMPTIONS

20% of the individual's disposable earnings for a 60-day period

COLLECTION AGENCY BOND & LICENSE

- Bond: No
- License: No
- Fee: No

STATE: TENNESSEE

INTEREST RATE

- Legal: 10%
- Judgment: 10% (or contract rate); varies with type of transaction

STATUTE OF LIMITATIONS (IN YEARS)

- Open Account: 6
- Written Contract: 6
- Domestic Judgment: 10
- Foreign Judgment: 10

BAD-CHECK LAWS (CIVIL PENALTY)

Treble damages up to $500 plus 10% interest and reasonable service charges, attorney's fees, and court costs.

GENERAL GARNISHMENT EXEMPTIONS

See federal law. Add $2.50 per week for dependent child under 16.

COLLECTION AGENCY BOND & LICENSE

- Bond:

  - $15,000, 1-4 employee
  - $20,000, 5-9 employee
  - $25,000, 10 or more

- License: Yes
- Fee:

  - $600 - Original
  - $350 - Renewal
  - $25 - Each Solicitor

- Exemption for out-of-state collectors: Contact state licensing authority. Out-of-state agencies may be exempt if they (1) maintain office in another state; (2) reside in a state that provides reciprocity; and (3) comply with provisions of licensing.

STATE: TEXAS

INTEREST RATE*

- Legal: 6% with agreement can charge up to 18%. Without agreement, statutory interest of 6% begins to run 30th day after becoming due
- Judgment: 10%

STATUTE OF LIMITATIONS (IN YEARS)

- Open Account: 4
- Written Contract: 4
- Domestic Judgment: 10 (Renewable)
- Foreign Judgment: 10 (Renewable)

BAD-CHECK LAWS (CIVIL PENALTY)

N/A

GENERAL GARNISHMENT EXEMPTIONS

100% of wages

COLLECTION AGENCY BOND & LICENSE

- Bond: Yes
- License: No
- Fee: No

*Always consult counsel to charge interest; Texas has very onerous usury laws & penalties.

STATE: UTAH

INTEREST RATE

- Legal: 7.35%
- Judgment: Contract rate or Federal Judgment Rate

STATUTE OF LIMITATIONS (IN YEARS)

- Open Account: 4
- Written Contract: 6
- Domestic Judgment: 8
- Foreign Judgment: 8

BAD-CHECK LAWS (CIVIL PENALTY)

Certified statutory bad-check notice must be sent. Amount due, interest, court costs, reasonable attorney's fees, plus $15 bad-check fee.

GENERAL GARNISHMENT EXEMPTIONS

$142.50 of disposable earnings for wages paid weekly.

COLLECTION AGENCY BOND & LICENSE

- Bond: $10,000
- License: Yes
- Fee: Varies by city and county

STATE: VERMONT

INTEREST RATE

- Legal: 12%
- Judgment: 12%

STATUTE OF LIMITATIONS (IN YEARS)

- Open Account: 6
- Written Contract: 6
- Domestic Judgment: 8
- Foreign Judgment: 8

BAD-CHECK LAWS (CIVIL PENALTY)

Court costs, amount of check, attorney's fees, damage of $50 (Notices required).

GENERAL GARNISHMENT EXEMPTIONS

75% of earning above minimum wage or what is necessary to live.

COLLECTION AGENCY BOND & LICENSE

- Bond: No
- License: No
- Fee: No

STATE: VIRGINIA

INTEREST RATE

- Legal: 8%
- Judgment: 9% or contract rate, whichever is higher

STATUTE OF LIMITATIONS (IN YEARS)

- Open Account: 3 last charge or payment
- Written Contract: 5
- Domestic Judgment: 20
- Foreign Judgment: 10
- Sales of goods under article 2 is 4 years

BAD-CHECK LAWS (CIVIL PENALTY)

Lesser of $250 or three times check amount

GENERAL GARNISHMENT EXEMPTIONS

See federal law.

COLLECTION AGENCY BOND & LICENSE

- Bond: $5,000
- License: Depends on Locality
- Fee: No

STATE: WASHINGTON

INTEREST RATE

- Legal: 12%
- Judgment: 12%

STATUTE OF LIMITATIONS (IN YEARS)

- Open Account: 3
- Written Contract: 6
- Domestic Judgment: 10
- Foreign Judgment: 10

BAD-CHECK LAWS (CIVIL PENALTY)

Lesser of check amount or 12% interest, collection costs up to $40. If taken to court, reasonable attorney's fees, 3 x value, or up to $300. Now have 6 years to enforce a bad check.

GENERAL GARNISHMENT EXEMPTIONS

Greater of 75% or $64 week (40 times the federal minimum hourly wage).

COLLECTION AGENCY BOND & LICENSE

- Bond: $6,000 general, $4,000 specialty
- License: Yes
- Fee:

    o $100 - Investigation
    o $100 - Original
    o $100 - Renewable
    o $50 - Branch Office

- Exemption for out-of-state collectors: Contact state authorities. Out-of-state agencies may qualify for lesser licensing fees. Out-of-state collectors are no longer required to have resident office and in-state trust accounts if they don't have in-state client. Bond is not required if held in home state.

STATE: WEST VIRGINIA

INTEREST RATE

- Legal: 6%
- Judgment: 10%

STATUTE OF LIMITATIONS (IN YEARS)

- Open Account: 5
- Written Contract: 10
- Domestic Judgment: 10
- Foreign Judgment: 10

BAD-CHECK LAWS (CIVIL PENALTY)

Amount due, service charge up to $10. If check is under $500.00 = misdemeanor. Over $500.00 = felony.

GENERAL GARNISHMENT EXEMPTIONS

See West VA code 38-5A-3. Employees withhold 20% of disposable income or 30x the minimum hourly rate, whichever is less. Other exemptions apply.

COLLECTION AGENCY BOND & LICENSE

- Bond: $5,000
- License: Yes - Franchise Reg. Cert.
- Fee: $15 Annual
- Exemption for out-of-state collectors: Contact state authorities. Some out-of-state agencies may be exempt if they are only collecting for out-of-state clients.

STATE: WISCONSIN

INTEREST RATE

- Legal: 5%
- Judgment: 12%

STATUTE OF LIMITATIONS (IN YEARS)

- Open Account: 6
- Written Contract: 6
- Domestic Judgment: 20
- Foreign Judgment: 20

BAD-CHECK LAWS (CIVIL PENALTY)

Amount of check plus actual damages plus exemplary damages up to treble the amount of the check. Limited to $300.

GENERAL GARNISHMENT EXEMPTIONS

80% of net pay.

COLLECTION AGENCY BOND & LICENSE

- Bond: $15,000 min.
- License: Yes
- Fee:

- o $1000 - Investigation
- o $200 - Annual

- Exemption for out-of-state collectors: Out-of-state agencies do not need to be licensed if (1) collecting by interstate means (phone, fax, mail) and (2) collecting for an out-of-state client.

STATE: WYOMING

INTEREST RATE

- Legal: 7%
- Judgment: Contract rate or 10% judgment rate

STATUTE OF LIMITATIONS (IN YEARS)

- Open Account: 8
- Written Contract: 10
- Domestic Judgment: 5
- Foreign Judgment: 5

BAD-CHECK LAWS (CIVIL PENALTY)

Double the face amount plus damages equal to collection cost and reasonable attorney fees.

GENERAL GARNISHMENT EXEMPTIONS

See federal law for consumer credit sale, lease, or loan. Up to 65% for child support arrearage.

COLLECTION AGENCY BOND & LICENSE

- Bond: $10,000
- License: Yes
- Fee:

  - o $200 - Original

- o $100 - Renewal
- o $100 - Branch

- Exemption for out-of-state collectors: Out-of-state agencies may bypass licensing if they are not (1) soliciting clients in Wyoming or (2) collecting for Wyoming creditors.

PUERTO RICO

INTEREST RATE

- Legal: 9.25% changes every 6 months (6/30/97)
- Judgment: It is regulated by the Commissioner of the Board of Financial Institutions every 6 months.

STATUTE OF LIMITATIONS (IN YEARS)

- Open Account: 3
- Merchandise Open Account: 3
- Written Contract: 15
- Mortgage: 20
- Domestic Judgment: 15
- Foreign Judgment: 15

BAD-CHECK LAWS (MISDEMEANOR)

See articles 1851-1856 of the Puerto Rico Penal Code regarding bad-check laws.

GENERAL GARNISHMENT EXEMPTIONS

75% of last 30 days' earnings for family support

COLLECTION AGENCY BOND & LICENSE

- Bond: $5,000
- License: Yes
- License Fee:

- o $100 - Original
- o $100 - Branch Office
- o $100 - Renewable
- o $100 - Investigation

(Source: http://carreonandassociates.com/articles/collectionlaws.htm)

CHAPTER 15

PAYDAY LOANS

In our opinion, payday loans are the worst possible loan that you could take out. It's a loan that you should stay away from. However, these days, payday loans have become extremely popular, and in fact, it would seem that everywhere you turn there is an offer for a payday loan to get you the extra money you need until the next payday. But are payday loans really a good idea? Sure, they can help you out when you're in a tight spot financially; however, there are several serious factors to consider before you actually take out such a loan.

First, let's look at how payday loans work. Usually the lender will agree to lend you a specified amount of money for a certain period of time. For example, let's say you needed $200 to cover some unexpected expenses. You would borrow the $200 and write out a postdated check for two weeks hence to cover the amount of the loan plus the finance fee, which would be around $60 for this size loan. So, in two weeks the lender expects to be able to cash that check for $260 to recoup the loan extended to you.

Before taking out the loan, it is extremely important to ask yourself whether you will really be able to afford to pay back the loan when it comes due. Most payday loans are made on a two-week to four-week basis. In the event that you can't pay back the loan at the end of that time frame, most payday loan companies will be quite happy to extend the loan; however, if you do that you will be charged more interest.

This brings up an interesting point because it can be difficult to determine how much interest you're paying on a payday loan when it involves numerous extensions. Depending on the number of extensions you take on the loan, you may actually be paying 300% interest, at a minimum. No, that's not a typo. How can they do that? Because there are no regulations regarding the amount of interest charged on payday loans when they are extended in this fashion. As you can well imagine, with this high interest rate, you may never be able to pay back the loan. And depending on how long you continue to extend the loan, you may actually end up paying far more than that rate. Based on our earlier example, if you extended the loan 3 months after the original due date, you would owe almost $500; more than double the amount you originally borrowed.

Other problems can be associated with taking out a payday loan too. For example, if you happen to unfortunately be working with a company that is less than scrupulous you may find yourself owing bounced check fees as well. You can occur additional fees if the lender deposits your postdated check before the agreed-upon date or if you don't have enough funds in your account to cover the check on the date you agreed upon.

Regulators of consumer protection groups are worried about how payday lenders operate. These lenders have very aggressive collection practices. The Federal Trade Commissions, Consumer Union, and Consumer Federation of America have all expressed concern about payday loans.

According to a study by Georgetown University researchers, cash-strapped consumers often roll over their payday loans multiple times and wind up paying more than 1,000% in interest.

When all factors are taken into consideration, payday loans can be a dangerous risk and should only be considered if you truly have no other alternatives, such as taking out a small loan from your bank or credit union, borrowing from family or friends, or simply making arrangements with your debtor to wait until you receive your next paycheck.

CHAPTER 16

NEGOTIATED SETTLEMENTS THAT HAVE BEEN ACCEPTED FROM CREDITORS, COLLECTION AGENCIES, AND ATTORNEYS

In this the final chapter, we are going to show you the impact debt settlement can have when done correctly. You will see several debt settlement success stories that were negotiated using the do-it-yourself debt settlement model outlined in Chapter 7.

We specifically chose settlements that were negotiated with:

- ➤ creditors
- ➤ attorneys representing creditors and/or debt buyers
  - ○ attorneys that have filed a lawsuit on behalf of the creditor
- ➤ collection agencies representing creditors and/or debt buyers
- ➤ debt buyers

The reason we did this was simple: we wanted you to see what is possible with debt settlement, and regardless who you are negotiating with, you can have success and obtain a very desirable settlement.

In this case from 2012, the Law Firm of Allan C. Smith, P.C., was representing the interest of debt buyer CACH, LLC, who purchased this debt from Citibank Trust and/or GE Money.

- The Debtor received a notice from the attorney and disputed the debt in its entirety. Additionally, the Debtor requested validation of the claimed debt amount. See the dispute letter below on this page.
- The law firm sent a validation notice to this Debtor that partially supported the debt claimed due. See this notice on page 206.
- The Debtor again disputed the claim. See this dispute letter on page 207.
- The Debtor did not receive a response from the second dispute letter and decided to propose a settlement offer for 30% of the claimed amount due, payable over 6 months. See proposal on page 208.
- The attorney agreed to the Debtor's terms. See on this letter on page 209. **This was a 70% balance reduction; the Debtor reduced their debt from $11,741.43 to $3,522, for a savings of $8,219.43.**

Law Firm of Allan C. Smith, P.C.
1276 Veterans Highway
Suite E-1
Bristol, PA 19007

Re: CACH, LLC   SENT VIA FAX: 215-428-0740
Your Acct #: ████████
Original Creditor:CITICORP TRUST BANK/GE MONEY
Original Balance: ███████████
Current Balance: $11,741.43

To whom it may concern:

I am in receipt of your correspondence dated May, 15, 2011. Your letter indicates that I have a past due balance due to your client CACH, LLC in the amount of $11,741.43. Please be advised that this debt is disputed in its entirety. Now therefore, am requesting that your firm provide me with the following documents:

1. Agreement with your client that authorizes you to collect on this alleged debt.
2. Agreement that bears my signature of the alleged debtor wherein I promises to pay the above named client/creditor.
3. Complete payment history on this account so as to prove that the debt amount you wish to collect is correct.
4. Verification that your client is the authorized Title Holder of this account
5. New Jersey License and/or Bond certificate authorizing you/your firm to collect a debt in the state of New Jersey.

Accordingly, under the Fair Debt Collection Practice Act (FDCPA) you must cease all collection activity and remove all negative reporting until validity of the debt is proven.

Be advised should any negative reporting to any of the credit bureaus appear on my credit report bearing your firms name and/or your clients, I will immediately pursue legal actions against Law Firm of Allan C. Smith, P.C. and CACH, LLC and CITIBANK TRUST for violation of the FDCPA and Fair Credit Reporting Act (FCRA).

Accordingly, should Law Firm of Allan C. Smith, P.C. pursue any collection activity against me regarding the above referenced matter, without first providing verification of the underlying debt will be a violation of the FDCPA. At which time I will aggressively pursue legal actions against Law Firm of Allan C. Smith, P.C. and CACH, LLC and CITIBANK TRUST for such violations.

Law Firm of Allan C. Smith, P.C.

The Bucks County Office Center
1276 Veterans Highway, Suite E-1
Bristol, Pennsylvania 19007
Toll Free (888) 275-6399
Fax (215) 428-0740

Allan C. Smith, Esq.
Admitted: PA and NY

Of Counsel.
Corryn Kronnagel, Esq.
Admitted: PA
Ashley Vaivada, Esq.
Admitted: NJ

July 9, 2012

RE:
Our Client:	CACH, LLC
Our File Numbe	
Original Creditor:	Citicorp Trust Bank
Original Account Number:	
Current Balance:	$11,741.43

Dear

Enclosed is the information you requested to validate the above account we are servicing.

As you know, this law firm has been retained to secure payment on this account upon receipt of the enclosed information. We need you to contact Donna Tate at this office to make arrangements for payment of the balance.

We appreciate your working with us to resolve this matter.

At this time, this law firm is acting solely as a debt collector and no attorney with this firm has personally reviewed the particular circumstances of your account.

This communication is from a debt collector in an attempt; any information obtained is used for that purpose.

Sincerely,

185

CHRISTOPHER KESSLER & MICHAEL MORTORANO

July 31, 2012

Law Firm of Allan C. Smith, P.C.
1276 Veterans Highway
Suite E-1
Bristol, PA 19007

Re: CACH, LLC   SENT VIA FAX: 215-428-0740
Your Acct #:
Original Creditor: CITICORP TRUST BANK
Original Balance:
Current Balance: $11,741.43

To whom it may concern:

I am in receipt of your correspondence dated July 9, 2012, as well as the 4 statements that you enclosed with your letter. Your letter indicates that I have a past due balance due to your client CACH, LLC in the amount of $11,741.43. Please be advised that this debt is disputed in its entirety. Now therefore, am requesting that your firm provide me with the following documents:

1. Agreement that bears my signature of the alleged debtor wherein I promises to pay the above named client/creditor.
    a. Receipt(s) of purchase(s) that bear my signature for the alleged goods/services totaling the alleged balance due.
2. Agreement with your client that authorizes you to collect on this alleged debt.
3. **Complete payment history on this account** so as to prove that the debt amount you wish to collect is correct.
4. Verification that your client is the authorized Title Holder of this account
5. New Jersey License and/or Bond certificate authorizing you/your firm to collect a debt in the state of New Jersey.

Accordingly, under the Fair Debt Collection Practice Act (FDCPA) you must cease all collection activity and remove all negative reporting until validity of the debt is proven.

Be advised should any negative reporting to any of the credit bureaus appear on my credit report bearing your firms name and/or your clients, I will immediately pursue legal actions against Law Firm of Allan C. Smith, P.C. and CACH, LLC and CITIBANK TRUST for violation of the FDCPA and Fair Credit Reporting Act (FCRA).

Accordingly, should Law Firm of Allan C. Smith, P.C. pursue any additional collection activity against me regarding the above referenced matter, without first providing verification of the underlying debt will be a violation of the FDCPA. At which time I will vigorously pursue legal actions against Law Firm of Allan C. Smith, P.C., CACH, LLC and CITIBANK TRUST for such violations.

Please be guided accordingly,

DIG YOURSELF OUT OF DEBT

October 27, 2012

Law Firm of Allan C. Smith, P.C.
1276 Veterans Highway
Suite E-1
Bristol, PA 19007

Re:	CACH, LLC	SENT VIA FAX: 215-428-0740
Your Acct #:		
Original Creditor:	CITICORP TRUST BANK	
Original Balance:		
Current Balance:	$11,741.43	

To whom it may concern:

* * * * 2ND NOTICE PROPOSING SETTLEMENT OFFER * * * *

Allan:

This is the second letter I am sending in response to your correspondence dated August 1, 2012, regarding the above referenced account. I would like to propose a settlement to satisfy the above referenced account.

I hereby notify you that I am not acknowledging or accepting that I owe this debt, as this debt has not yet been fully verified. Additionally, this letter does not imply a promise to pay the debt unless you provide a response as detailed below.

I am proposing a settlement offer in the amount of $3,522.00 payable in 6 equal monthly payments of $587.00 as payment of this debt in full.

If you find my offer acceptable, please send me a settlement letter/agreement agreeing to the terms. It will be convenient for me if the letter is signed by your authorized agent. The letter should be subject to the laws of my state and treated as a contract. Upon receipt, I shall wire/overnight/or pay with a check by phone my first payment in the amount $587.00.

As per the Fair Debt Collection Practices Act, I have the right to dispute this alleged debt. **In case I do not receive your postmarked response within 15 days of the date of this correspondence, I shall withdraw the offer and request full verification of this debt.**

This settlement proposal is being made in the spirit and context of settlement negotiations and without prejudice.

Please forward your agreement to my address listed above.

Law Firm of Allan C. Smith, P.C.

The Bucks County Office Center
276 Veterans Highway, Suite E-1
Bristol, Pennsylvania 19007
Toll Free: (888) 275-6399 Fax: (215) 428-0740

Allan C. Smith, Esq.
Admitted: PA and NY

Of Counsel:
Corryn L. Kronnagel, Esq.
Admitted: PA
Ashley N. Vaivada, Esq.
Admitted: NJ and PA

October 26, 2012

Midland Park, NJ 07432

RE: Our Account No.:
         Our Client: CACH, LLC
         Original Creditor: GE MONEY
         Original Account No.:
         Current Balance: $ 11,741.43

To Whom It May Concern,

This letter is to confirm your recent telephone conversation with our office on October 26, 2012 concerning the above-styled matter. It is accepted and agreed that you will remit a total of $ 3,522.00, in the following manner:_

Six Monthly Payments: $ 587.00   Due no later than: The 15th of each month November 2012-April 2013

We agree not to proceed in any manner for so long as your payments are on time, and are in the full agreed-upon amount(s). If you default we will do that which will best protect the interests of our client. You are advised, and should clearly understand that in the event of default, any interest, attorney fees or other charges permissible under the terms of any agreement signed by you, or applicable law, can be added. Upon receipt and clearance of ALL payments, your account will be marked "Settled in Full". If you have any questions, please feel free to contact my office at the above number.

Please make your check or money order payable to Law Firm of Allan C. Smith, P.C. and be sure to include your account number as shown above for proper credit. Please send payment to Bucks County Office Center, 1276 Veterans Highway, Suite E-1, Bristol, PA 19007, unless you have already made an arrangement with post dated checks on file. A request for a receipt must be accompanied with a stamped, addressed envelope. You may request a written statement not more than twice yearly, although feel free to call for a remaining balance anytime.

188

In this 2009 case, the Law Offices of Cohen & Slamowitz, LLP, is representing the interest of HSBC Bank of Nevada, N.A.

- The law firm filed a lawsuit against this Debtor.
- The Debtor contacted the law firm after they received the below summons and complaint and proposed a settlement offer of **$712.01.**
- The law firm accepted this settlement in writing. See this acceptance on page 213.
- This was a **51% balance reduction; the Debtor saved $729.01.**

11-16-'09 15:34 FROM-   T-249 P003/005 F-424

CONSUMER CREDIT TRANSACTION
IMPORTANT!! YOU ARE BEING SUED!! THIS IS A COURT PAPER - A SUMMONS DON'T THROW IT AWAY!! TALK TO A LAWYER RIGHT AWAY! PART OF YOUR PAY CAN BE TAKEN FROM YOU (GARNISHEED). IF YOU DO NOT BRING THIS TO COURT, OR SEE A LAWYER, YOUR PROPERTY CAN BE TAKEN AND YOUR CREDIT RATING CAN BE HURT!! YOU MAY HAVE TO PAY OTHER COSTS TOO!! IF YOU CAN'T PAY FOR YOUR OWN LAWYER BRING THESE PAPERS TO THIS COURT RIGHT AWAY. THE CLERK (PERSONAL APPEARANCE) WILL HELP YOU!! THIS COMMUNICATION IS FROM A DEBT COLLECTOR AND IS AN ATTEMPT TO COLLECT A DEBT. ANY INFORMATION OBTAINED WILL BE USED FOR THAT PURPOSE.

CIVIL COURT OF THE CITY OF NEW YORK,
COUNTY OF BRONX
---X
HSBC BANK NEVADA, N.A.
                    PLAINTIFF,
-AGAINST-

                    DEFENDANT(S).
---X

INDEX NUMBER
C&S FILE NO.

SUMMONS
PLAINTIFF'S ADDRESS
1111 TOWN CENTER DR
LAS VEGAS, NV 89134

THE BASIS OF THE VENUE DESIGNATED IS DEFENDANTS RESIDENCE

TO THE ABOVE NAMED DEFENDANT(S): YOU ARE HEREBY SUMMONED TO APPEAR IN THE CIVIL COURT OF THE CITY OF NEW YORK, COUNTY OF BRONX AT THE OFFICE OF THE CLERK OF THE SAID COURT AT 851 GRAND CONCOURSE, BRONX, NY 10451, IN THE CITY AND STATE OF NEW YORK, WITHIN THE TIME PROVIDED BY LAW AS NOTED BELOW AND TO FILE YOUR ANSWER TO THE ANNEXED COMPLAINT WITH THE CLERK: UPON YOUR FAILURE TO ANSWER, JUDGMENT WILL BE TAKEN AGAINST YOU FOR THE SUM OF $1,379.02 WITH INTEREST FROM October 2, 2009 TOGETHER WITH COSTS AND DISBURSEMENTS OF THIS ACTION.

DATED: October 9, 2009   COHEN & SLAMOWITZ, LLP, ATTORNEYS FOR PLAINTIFF
                    199 CROSSWAYS PARK DR., P.O. BOX 9004, WOODBURY, NY 11797-9004
                    (516) 686-8984; (800) 293-6006 ext. 8984; Refer to C&S File No. N291220

NOTE: THE LAW PROVIDES THAT (A) IF THIS SUMMONS IS SERVED BY ITS DELIVERY TO YOU PERSONALLY WITHIN THE CITY OF NEW YORK, YOU MUST APPEAR AND ANSWER WITHIN TWENTY DAYS AFTER SUCH SERVICE; OR (B) IF THIS SUMMONS IS SERVED BY DELIVERY TO ANY PERSON OTHER THAN YOU PERSONALLY, OR IS SERVED OUTSIDE THE CITY OF NEW YORK, OR BY PUBLICATION, OR BY ANY MEANS OTHER THAN PERSONAL DELIVERY TO YOU WITHIN THE CITY OF NEW YORK, YOU ARE ALLOWED THIRTY DAYS AFTER THE PROOF OF SERVICE THEREOF IS FILED WITH THE CLERK OF THIS COURT WITHIN WHICH TO APPEAR AND ANSWER.

DEFENDANT(S) TO BE SERVED:

CIVIL COURT OF THE CITY OF NEW YORK
COUNTY OF BRONX
--X
HSBC BANK NEVADA, N.A.
                PLAINTIFF,   INDEX NUMBER
-AGAINST-   FILE NO.

                                          COMPLAINT

                         DEFENDANT(S).
--X

      PLAINTIFF, BY ITS ATTORNEYS, COMPLAINING OF THE DEFENDANT(S), RESPECTFULLY ALLEGES THAT:

      1.   PLAINTIFF IS A NATIONAL BANKING ASSOCIATION ORGANIZED PURSUANT TO FEDERAL LAW. PLAINTIFF IS A DIRECT CREDITOR AND NOT A DEBT PURCHASER, AND AS SUCH IS NOT REQUIRED TO BE LICENSED BY THE DCA.

      2.   UPON INFORMATION AND BELIEF, THE DEFENDANT(S) RESIDES OR HAS AN OFFICE IN THE COUNTY IN WHICH THIS ACTION IS BROUGHT, OR THE DEFENDANT(S) TRANSACTED BUSINESS WITHIN THE COUNTY IN WHICH THIS ACTION IS BROUGHT, EITHER IN PERSON OR THROUGH AN AGENT AND THE INSTANT CAUSE OF ACTION AROSE OUT OF SAID TRANSACTION.

                   AS AND FOR A FIRST CAUSE OF ACTION

      3.   PLAINTIFF REPEATS AND REALLEGES EACH AND EVERY ALLEGATION CONTAINED IN THE FOREGOING PARAGRAPHS AS IF MORE FULLY SET FORTH HEREIN.

      4.   PLAINTIFF OFFERED TO OPEN A CREDIT ACCOUNT, ACCOUNT NO. 3743770016914270 (HEREINAFTER THE "ACCOUNT"), IN DEFENDANT'S NAME.

      5.   DEFENDANT ACCEPTED THE OFFER BY USING THE ACCOUNT.

      6.   DEFENDANT DEFAULTED BY FAILING TO MAKE PAYMENTS WHEN DUE.

      7.   DEMAND FOR PAYMENT OF THE ACCOUNT WAS MADE ON DEFENDANT, BUT DEFENDANT FAILED TO MAKE ALL THE REQUESTED PAYMENTS.

      8.   AFTER CREDITING DEFENDANT FOR ALL PAYMENTS AND CREDITS, THERE IS NOW DUE AND OWING BY DEFENDANT TO PLAINTIFF THE SUM OF $1,379.02, NO PART OF WHICH HAS BEEN PAID DESPITE DUE DEMAND THEREFOR.

AS AND FOR A SECOND CAUSE OF ACTION

9.   PLAINTIFF REPEATS AND REALLEGES EACH AND EVERY ALLEGATION CONTAINED IN THE FOREGOING PARAGRAPHS AS IF MORE FULLY SET FORTH HEREIN.

10.   THAT HERETOFORE, PLAINTIFF RENDERED TO DEFENDANT(S) A FULL AND TRUE ACCOUNT OF THE INDEBTEDNESS OWING BY THE DEFENDANT(S) AS A RESULT OF THE ABOVE AGREEMENT, IN AN AMOUNT AS HEREINABOVE SET FORTH WHICH ACCOUNT STATEMENT WAS DELIVERED TO AND ACCEPTED WITHOUT OBJECTION BY THE DEFENDANT(S) RESULTING IN AN ACCOUNT STATED IN THE SUM OF $1,379.02, NO PART OF WHICH HAS BEEN PAID DESPITE DUE DEMAND THEREFOR.

WHEREFORE, PLAINTIFF DEMANDS JUDGMENT AGAINST DEFENDANT(S) IN THE SUM OF $1,379.02 WITH INTEREST FROM October 2, 2009 TOGETHER WITH COSTS AND DISBURSEMENTS.

THE UNDERSIGNED ATTORNEY HEREBY CERTIFIES THAT, TO THE BEST OF HIS/HER KNOWLEDGE, INFORMATION AND BELIEF, FORMED AFTER AN INQUIRY REASONABLE UNDER THE CIRCUMSTANCES, THE PRESENTATION OF THE WITHIN COMPLAINT AND THE CONTENTIONS THEREIN ARE NOT FRIVOLOUS AS DEFINED IN PART 130-1.1 OF THE RULES OF THE CHIEF ADMINISTRATOR.

DATED: OCTOBER 9, 2009

YOURS, ETC.

191

Law Offices
Cohen & Slamowitz, LLP

(516) 686-8984
(800) 293-6006 ext. 8984
Fax 516 908-7993
Firm Representative:

199 Crossways Park Drive
P.O. Box 9004
Woodbury, NY 11797-9004

November 25, 2009

BRONX NY 10463-7801

    Re: Creditor: HSBC BANK NEVADA, N.A.
            Account No. XXXX-XXXX-XXXX-
            C&S File No.
            Index No.
            Balance Due as of November 25, 2009: $1,441.02

Dear

        Please be advised that my client agrees to accept the sum of $712.01 as settlement in full of the above referenced claim. Payment must be received by this office no later than November 25, 2009.

        If you should have any questions or comments, please feel free to contact me.

            Very truly yours,

THIS COMMUNICATION IS FROM A DEBT COLLECTOR AND IS AN ATTEMPT TO COLLECT A DEBT. ANY INFORMATION OBTAINED WILL BE USED FOR THAT PURPOSE.

LSIF

192

In this 2010 case, Forster & Garbus, LLC, a law firm is representing the interest of Citibank.

- The Debtor sent the below settlement offer outlining their hardship.
- Forster & Garbus, LLC, responded with an acceptance letter. See letter on page 215.
- This was a **49% balance reduction; the Debtor saved $1473.16.**

Forster & Garbus, LLC
PO Box 213
Farmingdale, NY 11735-0213

Sent Via Fax: **631-393-9490**

Re: ▮▮▮▮▮▮▮▮▮▮▮▮

Original Creditor:	CitiBank
▮▮▮▮▮▮▮▮▮▮	
Amount of claim:	$2,957.16
Settlement Offer:	$1,484.00

* * * * SETTLEMENT OFFER * * * *

To Whom It May Concern:

As you have been previously advised ▮▮▮▮▮▮▮▮▮▮▮▮▮▮▮▮▮▮▮▮. in an attempt to resolve the above referenced account(s) that is allegedly due. ▮▮▮▮▮▮▮▮ The following summarizes the hardship for ▮▮▮▮▮▮▮▮:

▮▮▮▮▮▮▮▮▮▮▮▮▮ *had a heart attack 14 months ago and suffers from coronary artery disease. Leukopeiai, hypertension and hyperlipidemial attached hereto, please find a letter dated October, 21, 2009 from* ▮▮ *doctor. Accordingly,* ▮▮ *is not employed and is not able to work at this time.* ▮▮ *is out of work due to a fire at a diner that she worked 4 days a week at. With her husbands medical condition it is doubtful that she will be able to return to work.*

▮▮▮▮▮▮▮▮ is trying to avoid filing for bankruptcy. Therefore; In the interest of the economy, and in light of our client's present cash flow, ▮▮▮▮▮▮▮▮ is willing to present a settlement proposal to resolve the above referenced account and avoid further expenses for all concerned. Please advise if you will accept our settlement offer of $1,484.00. This offer is submitted to you in the spirit and context of settlement negotiations and without prejudice.

I strongly urge you to consider the benefits of this settlement as opposed to the uncertainties and expense of continued collection efforts and/or possible litigation.

Please advise as to your position at your earliest possible convenience. Upon acceptance ▮▮▮▮▮▮▮▮ will make the appropriate financial arrangements for payment. Should you have any questions or comments, please do not hesitate to contact me toll free at ▮▮▮▮▮.

CHRISTOPHER KESSLER & MICHAEL MORTORANO

RONALD FORSTER - Adm. in NY Only
MARK A. GARBUS - Adm. in NY Only

EDWARD J. DAMSKY- Adm. in NY Only
GLENN S. GARBUS - Adm. in NY, NJ & CT
JOEL D. LEIDERMAN – Adm. in NY Only

FORSTER & GARBUS LLP
A NEW YORK LAW FIRM
500 BI-COUNTY BOULEVARD – SUITE 300
P.O. BOX 9030
FARMINGDALE, N.Y. 11735-9030
(631) 393-9400
Fax (631) 393-9490

TESS E. GUNTHER – Adm. in NY & CT
KRISTEN S. MANTYLA - Adm. in NY Only
MICHAEL J. FLORIO - Adm. in NY Only
ANNETTE ALTMAN - Adm. in NY Only
NILI FARZAN - Adm. in NY Only
TINA B. DAVIDSON - Adm. in NY Only
KEVIN M. KNAB – Adm. in NY Only

10/06/2010
Via Facsimile

FREEHOLD, NJ 07728

Re: CITIBANK (SOUTH DAKOTA), N.A.
Vs:
Account No:
Orig Acct#:
Ref No:
Orig Balance: $2,957.16

Dear Sir or Madam:

This will acknowledge that the above referenced account will be considered settled in full in the amount of $1,484.00. Payment is as follows: $494.66 due on 10/13/10, $494.66 due on 11/13/10, $494.68 due on 12/13/10.

This settlement will be null and void if this account is being paid from the proceeds of a sale of property or a refinance of property owned by the defendant.

A Stipulation of Discontinuance or a Satisfaction of Judgment, whichever is applicable, shall be filed with the CIVIL COURT OF THE CITY OF NEW YORK, COUNTY OF BRONX under index#   81081/10.

Make payment payable to "Citibank" and send to: Forster & Garbus LLP P.O. BOX 213, FARMINGDALE, NY 11735-9030.

Very truly yours,

FORSTER & GARBUS LLP

NYC Department of Consumer Affairs #1259596

In this 2011 case, the Law Firm of Zwicker & Associates P.C. is representing the interest of Kohl's and agreed to the Debtor's settlement offer of **$598.00**. This was a **45% balance reduction; the Debtor saved $488.43.**

From:Zwicker & Associates P.C.   978 686 3538   02/15/2011 16:12   #265 P.001/002

ZWICKER & ASSOCIATES, P.C.

ATTORNEYS AT LAW
80 Minuteman Road Andover, Massachusetts 01810
Tel. (877) 846-5051 / Fax (978) 686-3538
NY City Residents Only Call (877) 368-4531

THIS LAW FIRM EMPLOYS ONE OR MORE ATTORNEYS ADMITTED TO PRACTICE IN THE FOLLOWING STATES:

February 15, 2011

ARIZONA
CALIFORNIA
CONNECTICUT
FLORIDA
GEORGIA
IDAHO
ILLINOIS
KENTUCKY
MARYLAND
MASSACHUSETTS
MICHIGAN
NEW JERSEY
NEW HAMPSHIRE
NEW YORK
OHIO
OREGON
TENNESSEE
TEXAS
VIRGINIA
WASHINGTON
WEST VIRGINIA
DISTRICT OF COLUMBIA

RE: Kohl's

Account No.
Account Balance: $1,086.43

To whom it may concern:

This letter will confirm that our client, Kohl's, has agreed to accept $598.00 as settlement in full of the above-referenced account. This settlement is conditioned upon receipt by this office of a check in the amount of $598.00 on or before February 25, 2011.

Upon timely receipt of said payment and the successful negotiation thereof, this office shall advise our client that the account is settled in full. Thereafter, in due course, our client will notify the appropriate credit reporting agencies of the accounts settled status.

If the payment of the settlement amount is not made on or before the date stated above, acceptance of your settlement offer is withdrawn. If there are any questions or concerns please contact your account manager.

KB/EG/287/LB

1. This firm is a debt collector.
2. This firm is attempting to collect a debt and any information obtained will be used for that purpose.
3. Important notices appear on the back of this letter. Please read them as they may affect your rights.
4. Colorado residents: please read important notice on the back of this letter.

In this 2010 case, the Debtor negotiated a 60% balance reduction with Budzik & Dynia, LLC, a law firm representing the interest of First Premier Bank. Below you will see a settlement confirmation letter from Budzik & Dynia, LLC, agreeing to the proposed settlement. In this **60% balance reduction, the debtor saved $625.89.**

To: +1-7323036307   Page 2 of 2   2010-12-09 00:06:16 (GMT)   17734826200 From: Jeff Budzik

BUDZIK & DYNIA, LLC
Attorneys at Law
4849 N. Milwaukee Avenue, Suite 801
Chicago, Illinois 60630
Telephone: (773) 902-1130
Toll Free: (877) 867-9201
Web: www.budzikdynia.com

12/8/2010

SICKLERVILLE, NJ 080819538

Re: LVNV Funding LLC
      Reference #:
      Debt Balance: $1,043.15
      File #:
      Settlement Amount: $417.26

Dear

This letter is the proposed settlement agreement in response to your discussion with our office on 12/8/2010, regarding the above referenced debt to our client, LVNV Funding LLC. Our office has been authorized to accept $417.26 due on 12/10/2010 on behalf of our client, as settlement in full on this account.

Payments may be made through ACH, credit card, check or money order. If paying by ACH or credit card, in accordance with our agreement, payments will be processed by Budzik and Dynia, LLC on the above referenced dates. If paying by check or money order, please make payments payable to Budzik and Dynia, LLC and write your account number on the check or money order.

Failing to honor any of these stipulations will render this settlement offer null and void. Your balance will revert back to the original amount, less any payments made thereon.

Please be advised that our client may be required by law to report this settlement to one or more taxing authorities. The client makes no representation about tax consequences this may have or any reporting requirements that may be imposed on them. We advise that you consult an independent tax counsel of your own for any discussion on tax consequences which may result from this settlement.

Regards,

In this 2010 case, the Debtor negotiated a 60% debt reduction directly with World Financial Network National Bank. Below you will see a settlement confirmation letter from World Financial Network National Bank agreeing to the proposed settlement. In this **60% balance reduction, the Debtor saved $917.74.**

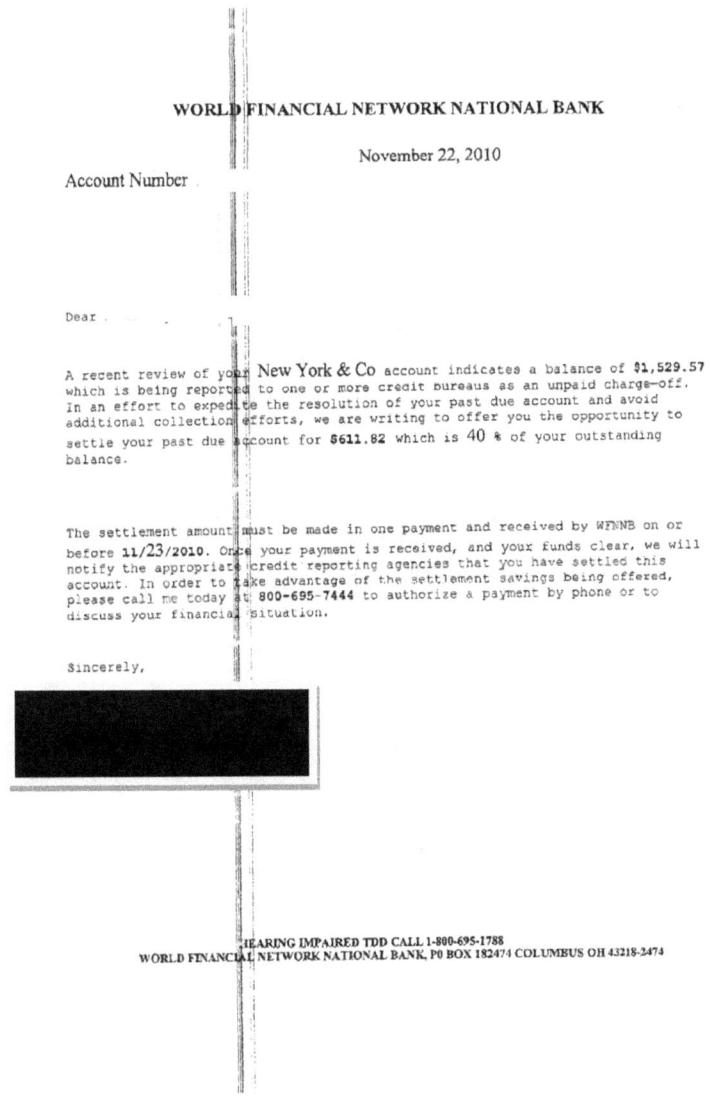

WORLD FINANCIAL NETWORK NATIONAL BANK

November 22, 2010

Account Number

Dear .

A recent review of your New York & Co account indicates a balance of $1,529.57 which is being reported to one or more credit bureaus as an unpaid charge-off. In an effort to expedite the resolution of your past due account and avoid additional collection efforts, we are writing to offer you the opportunity to settle your past due account for $611.82 which is 40 % of your outstanding balance.

The settlement amount must be made in one payment and received by WFNNB on or before 11/23/2010. Once your payment is received, and your funds clear, we will notify the appropriate credit reporting agencies that you have settled this account. In order to take advantage of the settlement savings being offered, please call me today at: 800-695-7444 to authorize a payment by phone or to discuss your financial situation.

Sincerely,

HEARING IMPAIRED TDD CALL 1-800-695-1788
WORLD FINANCIAL NETWORK NATIONAL BANK, PO BOX 182474 COLUMBUS OH 43218-2474

In this 2010 case, the Debtor negotiated a 50% balance reduction with Global Credit & Collections, a collection agency representing the interest of Capital One. Below you will see a settlement confirmation letter from Global agreeing to the proposed settlement. In this **50% balance reduction, the Debtor saved $763.36.**

GL BAL
CREDIT·COLLECTION CORP

GLOBAL CREDIT & COLLECTION CORP.
300 International Drive Suite 100
P.M.B 10015
Williamsville, NY 14221

PHILADELPHIA, PA
19103-7212

| Client: Capital One | Global ID: |
| Account #: ▉▉▉▉▉▉▉ | Amount: $1,526.71 |

November 22, 2010

Dear

This letter shall serve to confirm that Global Credit & Collection Corp. is the duly authorized agent acting on behalf of CAPITAL ONE. We are prepared to accept the sum of **$763.35** as final settlement of this account. Conditions of this settlement are as follows:

1) The payment of **$736.35** must be paid to Global Credit & Collection Corp. on or before 3pm before November 30, 2010.
2) Payments may not be returned by a financial institution for any reason.

If the conditions of this settlement are not met, this settlement will be considered null and void. If the terms of this settlement are met your Credit Bureau will be updated accordingly. A release letter will subsequently be provided.

Note: The internal Revenue Service requires the Creditor to provide it with information about amounts of $600.00 or more that are discharged as a result of a cancellation of debt If the amount the Creditor will discharge when the final payment of your settlement is received is $600.00 or more, the Creditor will be required to notify the IRS of the discharged amount. You will receive a copy of the form 1099C that will be filed with the IRS.

Yours truly,

▉▉▉▉▉▉▉▉▉▉▉

THIS HAS BEEN SENT TO YOU BY A DEBT COLLECTOR
This is an attempt to collect a debt. Any information obtained will be used for that purpose.

Global Credit & Collection Corp. *300 International Drive, Ste 100*, Williamsville, NY. 14221

In this 2010 case, the Debtor negotiated a 50% balance reduction with First National Collection Bureau, Inc., a collection agency representing the interest of Jefferson Capital Systems and Fingerhut. Below you'll see a settlement confirmation letter from National Collection Bureau, agreeing to the proposed settlement. In this **50% balance reduction, the Debtor saved $285.82.**

NOV-22-2010 13:46   From:775-322-0438   Page:2/2

FIRST NATIONAL COLLECTION BUREAU, INC

November 22, 2010

Sickerville, NJ 08081

CLIENT: Jefferson Capital Sys/Fingerhut
Account #:
Balance Due: $571.63
SIF Amount: $285.81
Due Date: 11/23/10

First National Collection Bureau Inc, as acting agent for Jefferson Capital Sys/Fingerhut, has agreed to accept $285.81 as settlement in full on the above referenced account.

This offer is only guaranteed if we receive your payment of $285.81 in our office on or before 11/23/10. If we do not receive the payment in full amount by that date, we reserve the right to modify the offer or revoke it in its entirety.

Upon clearance of your payment we will notify our client so it can update its records accordingly, as well as update the proper credit reporting agencies.

If you have any questions please contact us at 1-800-824-6191.

This is a communication from a debt collector. This is an attempt to collect a debt. Any information obtained will be used for that purpose.

In this 2010 case, the Debtor negotiated a 60% balance reduction with Pinnacle Financial Group, Inc., a collection agency representing the interest of First Premier Bank. Below you will see a settlement confirmation letter from Pinnacle agreeing to the proposed settlement. In this **60% balance reduction, the Debtor saved $323.54.**

11/22/2010 MON 17:50 FAX   @002/002

PINNACLE FINANCIAL GROUP, INC.
7825 Washington Avenue South • Suite 310 • Minneapolis, MN 55439

Nov 22, 2010

                                          ACCOUNT NUMBER:

SICKLERVILLE, NJ 08081

                    SETTLEMENT NOTICE

        Creditor   Account #   Amt Owed
FIRST PREMIER BANK   ████████████   549.23

This letter is to confirm your settlement of the above referenced account
for 219.69. This payment must be received in our office by 12/01/10
as we agreed. Upon receipt of this amount, your account will be Settled in
Full.

This letter and your cancelled check or other receipt will serve as your
proof of payment.

If you have any questions please call me at 1-877-209-4163   . Thank you
in advance for your desire to resolve this matter.
We are not obligated to renew this offer.

SINCERELY,

████████████████████████████

THIS LETTER IS AN ATTEMPT TO COLLECT A DEBT AND ANY INFORMATION OBTAINED
WILL BE USED FOR THAT PURPOSE.
THIS COMMUNICATION IS FROM A DEBT COLLECTOR.

In this 2009 case, the Debtor negotiated a 38% debt reduction directly with Chase. Below you will see a settlement confirmation letter from Chase agreeing to the proposed settlement. In this **38% balance reduction, the Debtor saved $1,541.45.**

CHASE ⬤

Cardmember Service
P.O. Box 15548
Wilmington, DE 19886-5548

BRONX NY 10463

Account:
BALANCE: $4056.44

Settlement Confirmation

Dear   :

We are pleased to confirm that we've agreed to settle your credit card account for $2500.00. Our settlement brings you these three advantages:

- You will pay $2500.00, a significant savings over the full balance that you owe us*.
- We will stop all efforts to collect.
- We will report your account to the national credit bureaus as "settled".

Here is your schedule of payment that you have agreed to:

Due Date: 08/31/2009   Payment Amount: $2500.00

Please call 1-800-848-1551 toll-free to make payment arrangements, or you can mail us your payment to the address below. For your convenience, your first payment due will be given a 10-day grace period from the due date listed above. We must receive your payment before your grace period expires, or before the date your account is scheduled to charge off, whichever comes first. If you have any questions about your settlement agreement or, want to find out your charge off date, please call us at 1-800-848-1551.

Until your settlement amount is paid in full, your Annual Percentage Rate will be 14.99%. This will have no impact on your settlement amount or payment(s). If you don't make each payment by its due date listed above, or we receive an insufficient payment (NSF), our settlement agreement will terminate and your account will revert to the terms of your Cardmember Agreement. If you are removed from the settlement plan, we'll continue our collection efforts and any payments made to that point would be applied to your full balance.

If you have not already done so, please destroy all the cards and convenience checks for your account as we have closed your account as part of the settlement agreement. We look forward to receiving your payment.

Sincerely,

P.S. Send your cashier's check or money order for your payment of ($2500.00) today to the address below.

Mail to: Cardmember Service
P.O. Box 15548
Wilmington, DE 19886-5548

Overnight address: Cardmember Service
Attn: Remittance Processing
2500 Westfield Drive
Elgin, IL 60123

* IRS requires us to provide them with information about certain amounts that are discharged as a result of a cancellation of a debt on a form 1099C. If we are required to notify the IRS, you will receive a copy of the form 1099C that is filed with the IRS.

Account is owned by Chase Bank USA, N.A.
Calls may be monitored and/or recorded to ensure the highest level of quality service.

In this 2009 case, the Debtor negotiated a 45% debt reduction directly with Chase. Below you will see a settlement confirmation letter from Chase agreeing to the proposed settlement. In this **45% balance reduction, the Debtor saved $7,095.**

CHASE

Date: **October 19, 2009**

Bronx, NY 10463

Dear: .

Fax#

Account No:

Account Balance: $15,766.66

This letter is to confirm that we will accept a payment in the amount of $8,672.00 to be received through electronic posting or by certified bank check as settlement in full on the above referenced account.

Payment must be received by **October 29, 2009**. If payment is made by certified bank check, please mail to:

CHASE BANKCARD SERVICES, INC.
Exception Payment Processing
201 N. Walnut Street
Wilmington, DE 19801
Mailstop: DE1-0153

Once your payment has posted, Chase will update your credit bureau rating to indicate that the balance has now been settled.

If payment is not received within the required time frame, this offer will no longer be considered valid. In addition, you are responsible for any tax liability associated with this transaction. Please speak with your tax advisor concerning any other tax questions.

If you have any questions, please do not hesitate to contact us at 800-327-4676. A Chase Representative is available to help you between the hours of 7:00 AM to 10:00 PM local time, Monday through Friday, Saturday 7:00 AM to 4:00 PM and Sunday, 8:00 AM to 9:00 PM.

Sincerely,

CLOSING THOUGHTS

We hope that you found this book educational. One thing is for certain: it is much more difficult getting out of debt than getting into debt. The good news is there are various options that you can choose that will allow you to pay down and eliminate your debt—better, faster, and cheaper.

We understand that the financial challenges that you are facing and will be facing throughout this journey may be very difficult and at times you may want to give up and quit. When you feel like that we ask you to stay true to the process and remember you are doing this for a lifetime of financial freedom for you and your family.

Michael and I wish you a great deal of success and ask that you keep track of your progress and let us know about your success and victories in conquering your debt. Share your story with us at mystory@digyourselfoutofdebt.net. With your permission we will post your success stories on our website, keeping your identity confidential of course. Your stories will help motivate others in achieving their financial goals too.

We wish each you a lifetime of financial freedom!

Christopher Kessler

APPENDIX A: MONTHLY EXPENSE PLANNING WORKSHEET

Monthly Expense Planning Work Sheet   Month:_____ Year:_____

Expenses Description	Weekly Estimate	Week 1 Actual	Week 2 Actual	Week 3 Actual	Week 4 Actual	Week 5 Actual
Mortgage/Rent Payment	$	$	$	$	$	$
HELOC/Second Mortgage	$	$	$	$	$	$
Property Tax	$	$	$	$	$	$
Homeowners Association Fee	$	$	$	$	$	$
Household Maintenance Cleaning Supplies, Home Repairs, Pool, Landscape, etc.	$	$	$	$	$	$
Groceries	$	$	$	$	$	$
Utilities Gas, Water, Sewer, Trash, Cable, Phone, etc.	$	$	$	$	$	$
Automobile Loan Payment(s)	$	$	$	$	$	$
Automobile Maintenance Car Repairs, Maintenance, Car Wash, etc.	$	$	$	$	$	$
Commuting Expense Gas, Tolls, Bus/Train/Subway Tickets, etc.	$	$	$	$	$	$
Insurance Home, Auto, Medical, Life, Dental, Vision, etc.	$	$	$	$	$	$
Unsecured Loans Credit Cards, Credit Lines, Dept. Stores Cards, etc.	$	$	$	$	$	$
Clothing & Personal Care Haircuts, Manicures, Tanning, Beauty Products, etc.	$	$	$	$	$	$
Entertainment Dining Out, Movies, Concerts, Plays, etc.	$	$	$	$	$	$
Dues & Subscriptions Union Dues, Books, Magazines, Hobbies, etc.	$	$	$	$	$	$
Personal Allowance 1 Spouse	$	$	$	$	$	$
Personal Allowance 2 Spouse	$	$	$	$	$	$
Personal Allowance 3 Child/Parent	$	$	$	$	$	$
Personal Allowance 4 Child/Parent	$	$	$	$	$	$
Personal Allowance 5 Child/Parent	$	$	$	$	$	$
Other	$	$	$	$	$	$
Totals	$	$	$	$	$	$

APPENDIX B: GROSS MONTHLY INCOME WORKSHEET

Gross Monthly Income Worksheet   Month: _____ Year: _____

Description of Income Source	Your Gross Income	Spouse/Partner Gross Income	Total Gross Income
Salary - Wages from Employment	$	$	$
Salary - Self Employment	$	$	$
Social Security	$	$	$
Social Security - Widow/Survivors Benefits	$	$	$
Pension Benefit	$	$	$
IRA Income	$	$	$
Veterans Pension	$	$	$
Annuity Income	$	$	$
Alimony	$	$	$
Child Support	$	$	$
Rental Property Income	$	$	$
Investment Income	$	$	$
Inheritance/Trust	$	$	$
Gifts	$	$	$
Other Income	$	$	$
Total Monthly Income	$	$	$

APPENDIX C: NET ANNUAL INCOME WORKSHEET

Annual Worksheet   Year: _____

Description of Income Source	Your Gross Income	Spouse/ Partner Gross Income	Income Withheld (Less Taxes)	Income Less Withholdings X Frequency	= Annual Net After Taxes
Example:	$2,500.00	2000.00	-$810.00	X12	$44,280.00
Salary - Wages From Employment	$	$	$	$	
Salary - Self Employment	$	$	$	$	
Social Security	$	$	$	$	
Social Security - Widow/Survivors Benefits	$	$	$	$	
Pension Benefit	$	$	$	$	
IRA Income	$	$	$	$	
Veterans Pension	$	$	$	$	
Annuity Income	$	$	$	$	
Alimony	$	$	$	$	
Child Support	$	$	$	$	
Rental Property Income	$	$	$	$	
Investment Income	$	$	$	$	
Inheritance/Trust	$	$	$	$	
Gifts	$	$	$	$	
Other Income	$	$	$	$	
Total Monthly Income	$	$	$	$	

APPENDIX D: MONTHLY BUDGET PLANNER

Monthly Budget Planner   Month: _____   Year: _____

CATEGORY	MONTHLY BUDGET AMOUNT	MONTHLY ACTUAL AMOUNT	DIFFERENCE
INCOME:			
Wages and Bonuses			
Interest Income			
Investment Income			
Miscellaneous Income			
Income Subtotal			
INCOME TAXES WITHHELD:			
Federal Income Tax			
State and Local Income Tax			
Social Security/Medicare Tax			
Income Taxes Subtotal			
Spendable Income			
EXPENSES:			
HOME:			
Mortgage or Rent			
Homeowners/Renters Insurance			
Property Taxes			
Home Repairs/Maintenance/HOA Dues			
Home Improvements			
UTILITIES:			
Electricity			
Water and Sewer			
Natural Gas or Oil			
Telephone (Landline, Cell)			
FOOD:			
Groceries			
Dining Out, Lunches, Snacks			
FAMILY OBLIGATIONS:			
Child Support			
Alimony			
Daycare, Babysitting			
HEALTH AND MEDICAL:			
Insurance (Medical, Dental, Vision)			
Unreimbursed Medical Expenses, Co-pays			
Fitness (Yoga, Massage, Gym)			

207

TRANSPORTATION:			
Car Payments			
Gasoline/Oil			
Auto Repairs/Maintenance/Fees			
Auto Insurance			
Other Transportation (tolls, bus, subway, taxis)			
DEBT PAYMENTS:			
Credit Cards			
Student Loans			
Other Loans			
ENTERTAINMENT/ RECREATION:			
Cable TV/Videos/Movies			
Computer Expense			
Hobbies			
Subscriptions and Dues			
Vacations			
PETS:			
Food			
Grooming, Boarding, Vet			
CLOTHING:			
INVESTMENTS AND SAVINGS:			
401(K) or IRA			
Stocks/Bonds/Mutual Funds			
College Fund			
Savings			
Emergency Fund			
MISCELLANEOUS:			
Toiletries, Household Products			
Gifts/Donations			
Grooming (Hair, Makeup, Other)			
Miscellaneous Expense			
Total Investments and Expenses			
Surplus or Shortage (spendable income minus total expenses and investments)			

APPENDIX E: NET WORTH BALANCE WORKSHEET

Net Worth Balance Worksheet

Assets	Liabilities
Liquid Assets (Use cash values for these items)	**Common Liabilities**
Cash: $_____	Car Payment (Balance Remaining): $____
Checking Account: $_____	Credit Card Balances: $_____
Savings Account: $_____	Cash Loans (Amount Owed): $_____
Money Market Accounts: $_____	**Installment Credit** (Use Remaining Balances)
Insurance Policy: $_____	Appliances: $_____
Securities (Use Present Market Value for these items)	Furniture: $_____
Stocks: $_____	Home Improvements Credit: $_____
Bonds: $_____	Mobile Home: $_____
Mutual Funds: $_____	Other Payment Plans Owed: $_____
Other Non-marketable investments	**Taxes Due:**
Annuities: $_____	Income Tax: $_____
IRAs: $_____	Property Tax: $_____
Pension Plan $_____	
Tax Shelters: $_____	**Net Worth**
Durable Goods (Use Resale Value)	Total Liabilities: $_____
Automobiles: $_____	**Total Assets:** $_____
Motorcycles: $_____	Total Liabilities:- $_____
Mobile Homes: $_____	**Total Net Worth:** = $_____
Collectables: $_____	
Furnishings: $_____	
Furniture: $_____	
Electronics: $_____	
Jewelry: $_____	
Furs: $_____	

Assorted Equipment (Home, Sports):$_____

Real Property (Actual Worth)

Primary Home: $_____Vacation Home: $_____Income Property: $_____

Receivables Loans (Owed to You): $_____ **Total Assets:** $

APPENDIX F: GOALS WORKSHEET

Goals:

Long-Term Goals (5-10 years)	ESTIMATED COST:	DATE TO ACHIEVE
	$	
	$	
	$	
	$	

Intermediate Goals (3-5 years)	ESTIMATED COST:	DATE TO ACHIEVE
	$	
	$	
	$	
	$	
	$	

Short-Term Goals (1-2 years)	ESTIMATED COST:	DATE TO ACHIEVE
	$	
	$	
	$	
	$	
	$	

APPENDIX G: COLLECTOR CALL LOG

The Call Log

	Creditor Name	Contact Person	Phone Number	Nature of Call	Date Called	Time Called
1.						
2.						
3.						
4.						
5.						
6.						
7.						
8.						
9.						
10.						
11.						
12.						
13.						
14.						
15.						
16.						
17.						
18.						
19.						
20.						
21.						
22.						
23.						

APPENDIX H: EXAMPLE CEASE AND DESIST LETTER

Cease & Desist

{Your_Name}
{Your_Address}
{YourCity}, {State} {Zip}
{Your_Phone}

Date {Date}

{Creditor/Collector's Name}
{Creditor/Collector's Address}

Re:	Account Number:	{Original_Creditor_Name}
	Account No:	{Account_Number}
	Balance Due:	{Balance}
	Proposed Settlement:	{Settlement_Offer}

To whom it may concern:

I am sending this letter to request that your office remove my phone numbers from your database and contact me through written correspondence **ONLY** if you must communicate with me. I will no longer be accepting phone calls from creditors and will only respond to written communications

As I have told you in numerous telephone conversations, I am unable to pay the above referenced debt due at this time. Multiple daily calls from your office will not help in any way to improve my current situation, or to resolve my debts. Calls of this nature simply create severe undue stress and compound the situation making it nearly impossible to remedy the debts in a more timely fashion. I fully understand my financial obligations to you and will attempt to make restitution to the best of my ability, as I do not wish to seek relief in Federal Bankruptcy Court.

Please be advised, I hereby assert my right under section 805-C of the Fair Debt Collection Practice Act, to request that you cease any further communication with me. This shall include, but shall not be limited to, my home, work, friends, family, and/or places of recreation, etc.

Sincerely,

APPENDIX I: SETTLEMENT PROPOSAL

Date

/CreditorName/
/CreditorAddress/
/CreditorCity/, /CreditorState/ /CreditorZip/

Sent Via Fax: <u>/CreditorFax/</u>

Re: Your Name:	/FirstName/ /LastName/
Original Creditor:	/OriginalCreditorName/
Reference#	/CreditorAccountNumber/
Account Number:	/CreditorAccountNumber/
Amount of Claim:	$/AmountOfClaim/
Settlement Offer:	/CurrentSettlementOfferDollar/

* * * * SETTLEMENT OFFER * * * *

To Whom It May Concern:

As I have previously informed you that due to my current financial troubles, my debt to income simply will not allow for payment in full on this account. I am desperately trying to avoid having to file for bankruptcy.

Therefore, in an attempt to resolve the above-referenced account due I am presenting a settlement proposal to resolve the above-referenced account and avoid further expenses for all concerned.

Please advise if you will accept our settlement offer of $/SettlementOfferDollar/. In the interest of the economy, and in light of my current present cash flow, I urge you to consider the benefits of this settlement as opposed to the uncertainties and expense of continued collection efforts and/or possible litigation.

This offer is submitted to you in the spirit and context of settlement negotiations and without prejudice.

Please advise me of your position at your earliest possible convenience. Upon acceptance, I will make the appropriate financial arrangements for payment.

Sincerely,

APPENDIX J: EXAMPLE SETTLEMENT AGREEMENT

Date

/CreditorName/
/CredContact/
/CreditorAddress/
/CreditorCity/, /CreditorState/ /CreditorZip/

Fax: /CreditorFax/

Re: Your Name: _____
    Creditor Name: _____
    Account Number: _____
    Amount of claim: _____
    Settlement Offer: _____

Dear /CreditorContact/:

I am pleased that we have found a settlement that works for /CreditorName/. This letter shall confirm I agree to send **/$Dollar Amount/** as "Payment in Full" to settle the balance due on the above-referenced account. Upon receipt of payment /CreditorName/ agrees to release all claims and liability, under the above-referenced account.

Within 10 days of receiving my payment in the amount of **/$Dollar Amount/,** /CreditorName/ will delete from my credit reports any negative references related to the above account, and will update its records with the credit bureaus to reflect my account has been closed, upon conclusion of the "Paid in Full" or "Paid as Agreed" Account Closed.

Your signature below will verify your acceptance of these terms. Upon receipt of your executed copy of this agreement I will immediately forward my payment to you in the amount of /$Dollar Amount/.

This offer is submitted to you in the spirit and context of settlement negotiations and without prejudice.

Sincerely,

_____

Your Name

_____   ____/____/____

Creditor's Authorized Signature:

APPENDIX K: EXAMPLE OUT OF STAT LETTER

Date

/CreditorName/
/CredContact/
/CreditorAddress/
/CreditorCity/, /CreditorState/ /CreditorZip/

Fax: /CreditorFax/

Re: Your Name: _____
     Creditor Name: _____
     Account Number: _____
     Amount of Claim: _____
     Settlement Offer: _____

Dear /CreditorContact/:

This letter is response to your **phone call on/letter dated/, 201_**, concerning the above-referenced account number.

I have checked with my State Attorney General and confirmed that the statute of limitations on this type of debt has expired. Therefore, if you choose to pursue this matter in court, I will be forced to show proof that the statute of limitations has expired.

Let this letter serve as notification that I do not wish to be contacted about this debt any further except to be notified that future collection efforts are terminated. Any other communication regarding this debt will be taken as a violation of the Fair Debt Collection Practices Act.

Sincerely,

APPENDIX L: DISPUTE LETTER

Date

/CreditorName/
/CredContact/
/CreditorAddress/
/CreditorCity/, /CreditorState/ /CreditorZip/

Fax: /CreditorFax/

Re: Your Name: _____
    Creditor Name: _____
    Account Number: _____
    Amount of Claim: _____
    Settlement Offer: _____

Dear /CreditorContact/:

I am in receipt of your correspondence dated **/LetterDate/.** Your letter indicates that I have a past due balance due to your client **/CreditorName/** in the amount of **/$Amount/** Please be advised that this debt is disputed in its entirety. Now therefore, am requesting that your firm provide me with the following documents:

1. Agreement with your client that authorizes you to collect on this alleged debt.
2. Agreement that bears my signature of the alleged debtor wherein I promises to pay the above named client/creditor.
3. Complete payment history on this account so as to prove that the debt amount you wish to collect is correct.
4. Verification that your client is the authorized Title Holder of this account
5. **/YourState/** License and/or Bond certificate authorizing you/your firm to collect a debt in the state of **/YourState/**.

Accordingly, under the Fair Debt Collection Practice Act (FDCPA) you must cease all collection activity and remove all negative reporting until validity of the debt is proven.

Be advised should any negative reporting to any of the credit bureaus appear on my credit report bearing your firms name and/or your clients, I will immediately pursue legal actions against you and your client for violation of the FDCPA and Fair Credit Reporting Act (FCRA).

Accordingly, should you pursue any collection activity against me regarding the above referenced matter, without first providing verification of the underlying debt; that will be a violation of the FDCPA. At which time I will aggressively pursue legal actions against you and your client for such violations.

Please be guided accordingly,

Index

Notes

Notes

www.ingramcontent.com/pod-product-compliance
Lightning Source LLC
Chambersburg PA
CBHW072032190526
45165CB00017B/265